この本の特長と使い方

★このドリルは、1回分が、1枚の表と裏になっています。
★1回分は50点満点です。10分以内を目標に取り組みましょう。

表のページ

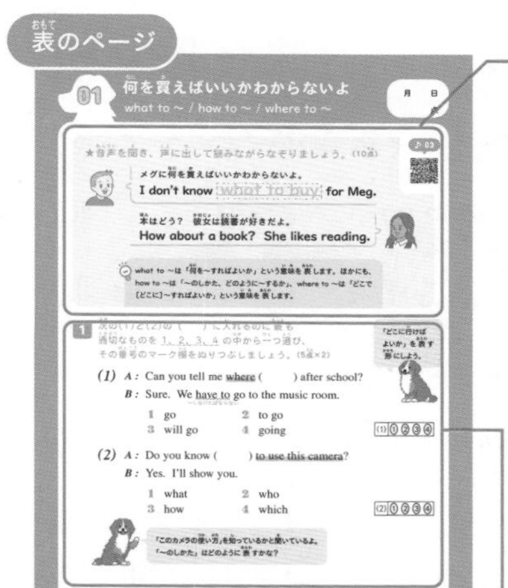

1 ウォーミングアップ

英検®でよく出る表現を、会話形式で紹介しています。
音声を聞き、声に出して読みながらなぞりましょう。

[音声の聞き方]

①各ページの二次元コードから聞く

インターネットに接続されたスマートフォンやタブレットで再生できます。

※通信料はお客様のご負担となります。

②音声再生アプリ「my-oto-mo(マイオトモ)」で聞く

右の二次元コードか、以下のURLにスマートフォンまたはタブレットでアクセスし、ダウンロードしてください。

https://gakken-ep.jp/extra/myotomo/

※通信料はお客様のご負担となります。　※パソコンからはご利用になれません。　※お客様のネット環境やご利用の端末により音声の再生やアプリの利用ができない場合、当社は責任を負いかねます。

裏のページ

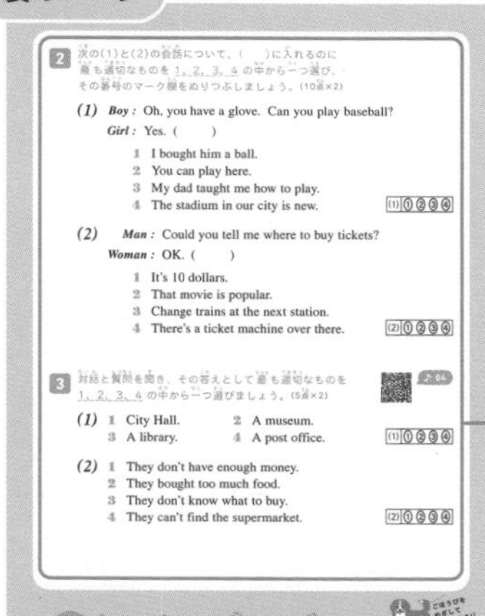

2 練習問題

英検®でよく出る表現を含んだ練習問題です。

※実際の試験問題より、英文が比較的短くなっています。難しいと感じたら、以下のヒントを見ながら取り組みましょう。

- 問題を解く時に注目すべき場所にオレンジ下線付き。
- キャラクターのサポート付き。
- 難しい単語や熟語の日本語訳付き。

3 実践問題

実際の英検®の試験形式に準じた問題です。英検®3級一次試験の大問1・2、リスニングテスト第1～3部のうち、2・3種類の形式で出題しています。表のページで勉強したことを思い出しながら取り組みましょう。

★**おさらいテスト** … 1つ前の級(4級)の問題を、実際の英検®の試

★**単語ページ** … 5、10、15、20、25、30回の計6回は、英検®3級

★**まとめテスト** … 実際の英検®の試験形式で、ジャンル別の予想

英検®は、公益財団法人 日本英語検定協会の登録商標です。
このコンテンツは、公益財団法人 日本英語検定協会の承認や推奨、その他の検討を受けたものではありません。

もくじ

★答えは、この本の最後にあります。

英検®受験ガイド

英検®は、文部科学省後援の検定試験で、
入試などでも評価されています。
ここでは、英検®3級を受験するみなさんのために、
申し込み方法や試験の行われ方などのお役立ち情報を紹介します。

3級の試験はこう行われる!

一次試験は筆記とリスニング

3級の一次試験は、2024年度から筆記65分、リスニング約25分の合計約90分で行われる予定※です。
ライティング問題以外、解答はすべてマークシート方式です。
※本書の情報は2023年7月現在のものです。

自宅の近くや学校で受けられる

一次試験は、全国の多くの都市で実施されています。
だいたいは、自宅の近くの会場や、自分の通う学校などで受けられます。

試験は年3回行われる

一次試験（本会場）は、
6月（第1回）・10月（第2回）・1月（第3回）の年3回行われます。
申し込みの受付の締め切りは、試験日のおよそ1か月前です。

二次試験（面接）について

一次試験に合格した人が受ける二次試験は、一次試験の約1か月後に実施されます。一次試験では問われないスピーキングの実力を問う試験です。

試験の申し込み方法は？

英検®の申し込み方法は、学校や塾の先生を通じて
まとめて申し込んでもらう団体申し込みと、
自分で書店などに行って手続きする個人申し込みの2通りがあります。
小・中学生の場合は、団体申し込みをして、
自分の通う学校や塾などで受験することが多いです。

まず先生に聞いてみよう

小・中学生の場合は、自分の通っている学校や塾を通じて団体申し込みをする場合が多いので、まずは担任の先生や英語の先生に聞いてみましょう。
団体本会場（公開会場）申し込みの場合は、
先生から願書（申し込み用紙）を入手します。
必要事項を記入した願書と検定料は、先生を通じて送ってもらいます。
試験日程や試験会場なども担当の先生の指示に従いましょう。

個人で申し込む場合はネット・コンビニ・書店で

個人で受験する場合は、次のいずれかの方法で申し込みます。

▶インターネット

英検®のウェブサイト（https://www.eiken.or.jp/eiken/）から申し込む。

▶コンビニエンスストア

店内の情報端末機から直接申し込む。
（くわしくは英検®のウェブサイトをご覧ください。）

▶書店

英検®特約書店（受付期間中に英検のポスターが掲示されています）に
検定料を払い込み、「書店払込証書」と「願書」を英検®協会へ郵送する。

申し込みなどに関するお問い合わせは、
英検®を実施している公益財団法人 日本英語検定協会まで。

- 英検®ウェブサイト　https://www.eiken.or.jp/eiken/
- 英検®サービスセンター　☎03-3266-8311

※英検®ウェブサイトでは、試験に関する情報・入試活用校などを公開しています。

本番のスケジュール

1 受付

受付で一次受験票兼本人確認票と身分証明書を見せます。（個人受験の場合）

↓

2 教室へ移動

自分の受験する教室を確認し、着席します。
受験番号によって教室がちがうので、よく確認しましょう。

↓

3 問題冊子と解答用紙の配布

受験者心得の放送に従って、解答用紙に必要事項を記入しましょう。

↓

4 試験開始

試験監督の合図で筆記試験開始です。

☑ 持ち物チェックリスト

● 必ず持っていくもの

- ☐ 一次受験票兼本人確認票
- ☐ 身分証明書
- ☐ HBの黒鉛筆やシャープペンシル（ボールペンは不可）
- ☐ 消しゴム

● 必要に応じて持っていくもの

- ☐ 腕時計（携帯電話・スマートフォンでの代用は不可）
- ☐ ハンカチ
- ☐ ティッシュ
- ☐ 防寒用の服
- ☐ 上ばき

おさらいテスト❶

月　日

点

1 次の(1)から(4)までの（　　）に入れるのに最も適切なものを 1、2、3、4 の中から一つ選び、その番号のマーク欄をぬりつぶしなさい。(5点×4)

空所の前に was があるね。

(1) ***A*:** Luke, where were you?

***B*:** In the library. I was (　　　) my homework.

1 do　　**2** did

3 doing　　**4** to do

(1) ① ② ③ ④

(2) ***A*:** I want a new bike.

***B*:** Look. My bike is (　　　) than yours.

1 old　　**2** older

3 oldest　　**4** best

(2) ① ② ③ ④

(3) Kenta had to (　　　) home early yesterday because his mother was sick.

1 go　　**2** goes

3 going　　**4** went

(3) ① ② ③ ④

(4) ***A*:** Did you have a good time at the party?

***B*:** Yes. I enjoyed (　　　) with my friends.

1 sing　　**2** singing

3 to sing　　**4** sang

(4) ① ② ③ ④

「私は友達と歌うことを楽しみました。」という文だよ。
空所には「歌うこと」を表すものが入るよ。
空所の前の enjoyed に注意。

2 次の(1)から(3)までの会話について、(　　)に入れるのに最も適切なものを 1、2、3、4 の中から一つ選び、その番号のマーク欄をぬりつぶしなさい。(6点×3)

(1) ***Son :*** I drew this picture for Grandma.

Mother : Wow, you're good at drawing. (　　　)

1 I won't call her.　**2** It looks really nice.
3 She needs some help.　**4** It's on the wall.

(1) ① ② ③ ④

(2) ***Girl 1 :*** It's nearly 5:00.

Girl 2 : Oh, (　　　) I'll make dinner with Dad today.

1 I like your watch.　**2** we were running.
3 you can't do it.　**4** I must go.

(2) ① ② ③ ④

(3) ***Woman :*** What do you want to do this afternoon?

Man : Well, (　　　)

Woman : Sounds nice.

1 How many do you want?　**2** How long was it?
3 How about watching a movie?　**4** How did you come?

(3) ① ② ③ ④

3 イラストを参考にしながら対話と応答を聞き、最も適切な応答を 1、2、3 の中から一つ選びなさい。(6点×2)

♪ 01

(1)

(1) ① ② ③

(2)

(2) ① ② ③

おさらいテスト❷

月　日

点

1 次の(1)から(4)までの（　　）に入れるのに最も適切なものを 1、2、3、4 の中から一つ選び、その番号のマーク欄をぬりつぶしなさい。(5点×4)

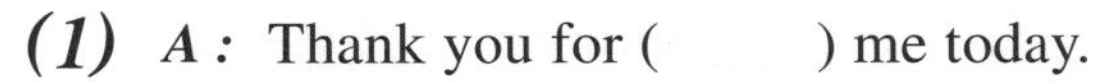

(1) ***A :*** Thank you for (　　　) me today.

B : You’re welcome.

1 helped　　**2** helping
3 to help　　**4** help

(1) ①②③④

(2) Lisa was happy (　　　) her old friend at the station.

1 to meet　　**2** met
3 meets　　**4** meet

(2) ①②③④

(3) ***A :*** Can you speak French?

B : Yes, a little. I lived in Paris (　　　) I was a child.

1 if　　**2** when
3 who　　**4** because

(3) ①②③④

(4) ***A :*** There are a lot of beautiful pictures in this museum.

B : Yeah. I think this one is the (　　　) of all.
I really like it.

1 good　　**2** better
3 best　　**4** more

(4) ①②③④

「この絵がすべての中で～と思う。」と言っているよ。
すぐ後の文から、とても気に入っているとわかるね。

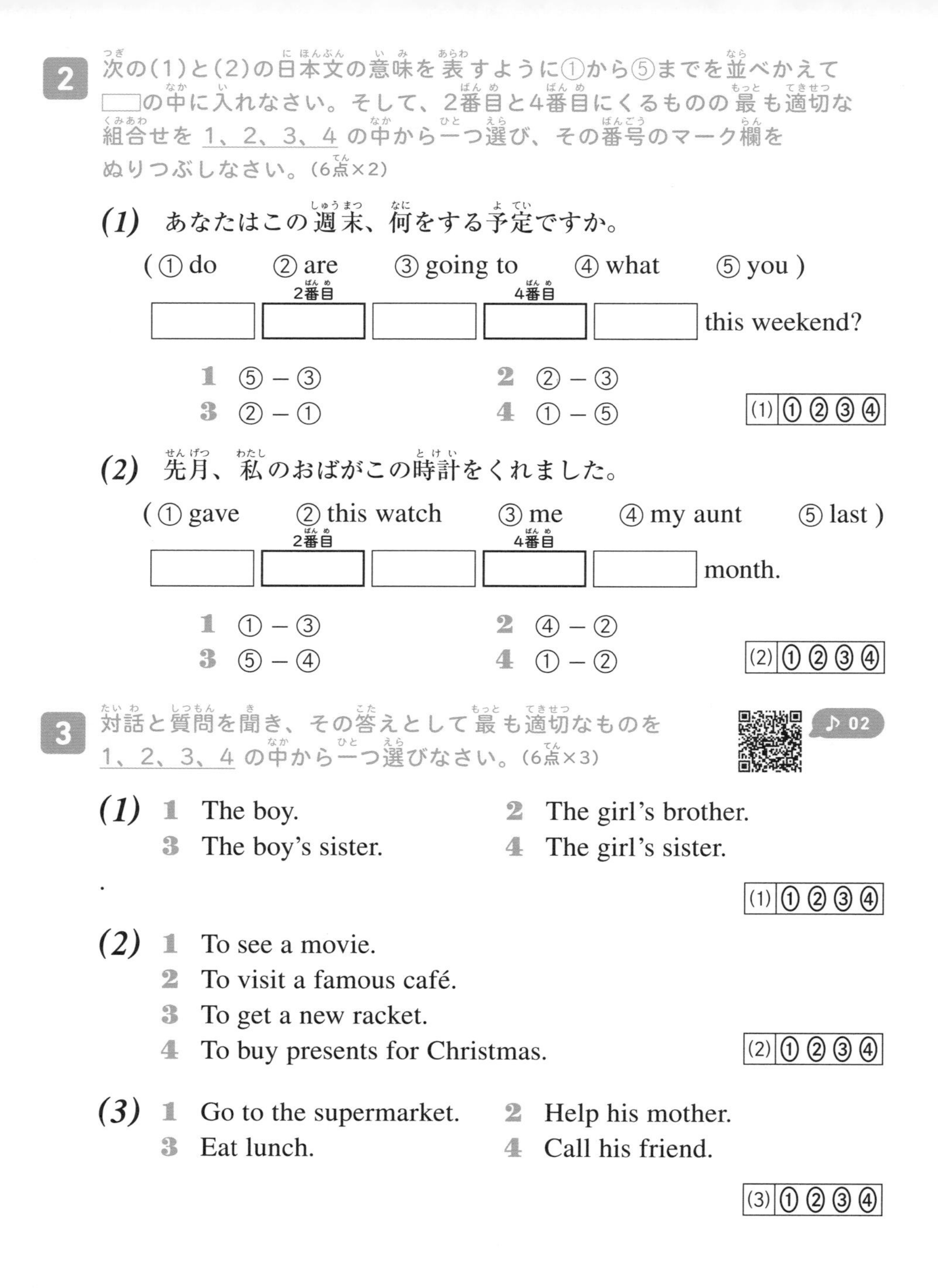

2 次の(1)と(2)の日本文の意味を表すように①から⑤までを並べかえて□の中に入れなさい。そして、2番目と4番目にくるものの最も適切な組合せを 1、2、3、4 の中から一つ選び、その番号のマーク欄をぬりつぶしなさい。(6点×2)

(1) あなたはこの週末、何をする予定ですか。

(① do ② are ③ going to ④ what ⑤ you)

□ □(2番目) □ □(4番目) □ this weekend?

1 ⑤ − ③　　2 ② − ③
3 ② − ①　　4 ① − ⑤

(1) ① ② ③ ④

(2) 先月、私のおばがこの時計をくれました。

(① gave ② this watch ③ me ④ my aunt ⑤ last)

□ □(2番目) □ □(4番目) □ month.

1 ① − ③　　2 ④ − ②
3 ⑤ − ④　　4 ① − ②

(2) ① ② ③ ④

3 対話と質問を聞き、その答えとして最も適切なものを 1、2、3、4 の中から一つ選びなさい。(6点×3)

♪ 02

(1)
1 The boy.
2 The girl's brother.
3 The boy's sister.
4 The girl's sister.

(1) ① ② ③ ④

(2)
1 To see a movie.
2 To visit a famous café.
3 To get a new racket.
4 To buy presents for Christmas.

(2) ① ② ③ ④

(3)
1 Go to the supermarket.
2 Help his mother.
3 Eat lunch.
4 Call his friend.

(3) ① ② ③ ④

01 何を買えばいいかわからないよ

what to ～ / how to ～ / where to ～

月　日
点

★音声を聞き、声に出して読みながらなぞりましょう。(10点)

メグに何を買えばいいかわからないよ。
I don't know what to buy for Meg.

本はどう？　彼女は読書が好きだよ。
How about a book? She likes reading.

what to ～は「何を～すればよいか」という意味を表します。ほかにも、how to ～は「～のしかた、どのように～するか」、where to ～は「どこで[どこに]～すればよいか」という意味を表します。

1 次の(1)と(2)の(　　)に入れるのに最も適切なものを 1、2、3、4 の中から一つ選び、その番号のマーク欄をぬりつぶしましょう。(5点×2)

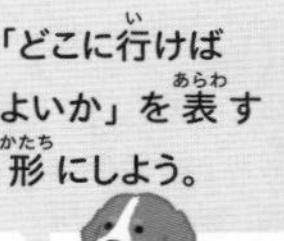

(1) **A:** Can you tell me where (　　　) after school?
B: Sure. We have to go to the music room.
(have to：～しなければならない)

1 go　　**2** to go
3 will go　　**4** going

(1) ① ② ③ ④

(2) **A:** Do you know (　　　) to use this camera?
B: Yes. I'll show you.

1 what　　**2** who
3 how　　**4** which

(2) ① ② ③ ④

「このカメラの使い方」を知っているかと聞いているよ。
「～のしかた」はどのように表すかな？

2 次の(1)と(2)の会話について、(　　)に入れるのに最も適切なものを 1、2、3、4 の中から一つ選び、その番号のマーク欄をぬりつぶしましょう。(10点×2)

(1) ***Boy :*** Oh, you have a glove. Can you play baseball?

Girl : Yes. (　　　)

1 I bought him a ball.
2 You can play here.
3 My dad taught me how to play.
4 The stadium in our city is new.

(1) ① ② ③ ④

(2) ***Man :*** Could you tell me where to buy tickets?

Woman : OK. (　　　)

1 It's 10 dollars.
2 That movie is popular.
3 Change trains at the next station.
4 There's a ticket machine over there.

(2) ① ② ③ ④

3 対話と質問を聞き、その答えとして最も適切なものを 1、2、3、4 の中から一つ選びましょう。(5点×2)

♪ 04

(1) **1** City Hall. **2** A museum.
3 A library. **4** A post office.

(1) ① ② ③ ④

(2) **1** They don't have enough money.
2 They bought too much food.
3 They don't know what to buy.
4 They can't find the supermarket.

(2) ① ② ③ ④

02 カレーを料理するのは簡単だよ
It's … (for —) to ～.

月　日
点

♪ 05

★音声を聞き、声に出して読みながらなぞりましょう。(10点)

きみがこのカレーを作ったの？
Did you make this curry?

うん！　カレーを料理するのは簡単だよ。
Yes! It's easy to cook curry.

It's[It is] easy to ～. は「～することは簡単です。」という意味を表します。「私にとって簡単」と言いたい場合は It's easy for me to ～. と表します。easy のほか、good(よい)、hard(大変な)などさまざまな様子を表す語が使われます。

1 次の(1)と(2)の（　　）に入れるのに最も適切なものを 1、2、3、4 の中から一つ選び、その番号のマーク欄をぬりつぶしましょう。(5点×2)

(1) (　　　) is interesting to read books.
おもしろい

1 This　　2 That
3 It　　4 I

(1) ① ② ③ ④

「～することはおもしろいです。」という文にしよう。

(2) It's difficult (　　　) me to swim fast.
難しい

1 over　　2 from
3 by　　4 for

(2) ① ② ③ ④

「速く泳ぐことは私にとって難しいです。」という文にしよう。
「私にとって」はどのように表すかな？

2 次の（　　）に入れるのに最も適切なものを1、2、3、4の中から一つ選び、その番号のマーク欄をぬりつぶしましょう。（10点）

A : I didn't have breakfast this morning.

B : Oh, it's important (　　　) breakfast.

1 have　　**2** had
3 to have　　**4** has

①②③④

3 次の会話について、（　　）に入れるのに最も適切なものを1、2、3、4の中から一つ選び、その番号のマーク欄をぬりつぶしましょう。（10点）

Girl : Eric, you're late. Did you get up late again?

Boy : Yeah. (　　　)

1 I went to bed early last night.
2 It's hard for me to get up early.
3 The bus didn't come on time.
4 I arrived here just before you came.

①②③④

4 対話と質問を聞き、その答えとして最も適切なものを1、2、3、4の中から一つ選びましょう。（5点×2）

♪ 06

(1) **1** To speak English.
2 To write stories.
3 To read English.
4 To play music.

(1) ①②③④

(2) **1** It's cool.　　**2** It's popular.
3 It's easy.　　**4** It's exciting.

(2) ①②③④

ごほうびをめざしてがんばろう!!

03 重すぎて運べないよ

too … to ～

月　日

点

★音声を聞き、声に出して読みながらなぞりましょう。(10点)

この箱は重すぎて運べないよ。

This box is too heavy to carry.

わかった。手伝うよ。

OK. I'll help you.

too heavy to carry は「重すぎて運べない」という意味を表します。「重すぎて私には運べない」と言いたい場合は too heavy for me to carry と表します。

1 次の(1)と(2)の（　　）に入れるのに最も適切なものを 1、2、3、4 の中から一つ選び、その番号のマーク欄をぬりつぶしましょう。(5点×2)

(1) I'm (　　　) tired to run.

tired: つかれて

1 very　　2 too
3 much　　4 hard

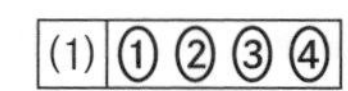

「～すぎる」を表す語が入るよ。

(2) This tea is too hot for me (　　　).

1 drinking　　2 drink
3 will drink　　4 to drink

(2) ① ② ③ ④

「このお茶は熱すぎて私には飲めません。」という文にするよ。
too hot (熱すぎる) があるから、どんな語句が入るかな？

2 次の(1)と(2)の会話について、(　　)に入れるのに最も適切なものを 1、2、3、4 の中から一つ選び、その番号のマーク欄をぬりつぶしましょう。(10点×2)

(1) ***Boy :*** How about this book for your brother?

Girl : (　　　) He's too young to read it.

1 It looks really nice.
2 Hmm, I think I'll buy something else.
3 I often go to the library with him.
4 OK, you can try again.

(1) ① ② ③ ④

(2) ***Father :*** Emma, can you come and cut these vegetables?

Daughter : Sorry, (　　　)

1 I'm good at cooking.
2 I can't go to the store.
3 I'm too busy to help you.
4 I didn't call Mom.

(2) ① ② ③ ④

3 英文と質問を聞き、その答えとして最も適切なものを 1、2、3、4 の中から一つ選びましょう。(5点×2)

♪ 08

(1)
1 He enjoyed fishing.
2 He played beach volleyball.
3 He swam in the sea.
4 He walked with his friends.

(1) ① ② ③ ④

(2)
1 She isn't good at math.
2 Her brother didn't help her.
3 She was too sleepy.
4 It was very difficult.

(2) ① ② ③ ④

ごほうびを めざして がんばろう!!

04 ギターをひいてほしい

want … to ～ / tell … to ～ / ask … to ～

月　　日

点

★音声を聞き、声に出して読みながらなぞりましょう。(10点)

あなたにギターをひいてほしいな。

I want you to play the guitar.

いいよ。何をひこうか。

OK. What should I play?

want 人 to ～は「(人)に～してほしい」という意味を表します。
tell 人 to ～は「(人)に～するように言う」、ask 人 to ～は「(人)に～するようにたのむ」という意味を表します。

1 次の(1)と(2)の (　　) に入れるのに最も適切なものを 1、2、3、4 の中から一つ選び、その番号のマーク欄をぬりつぶしましょう。(5点×2)

(1) I asked him (　　　) the rules.

たのんだ　ルール

1	explaining	**2**	explained
3	to explain	**4**	explains

(1) ① ② ③ ④

「ルールを説明するようにたのんだ」という文だよ。

(2) My mother (　　　) me to clean my room.

そうじする

1	said	**2**	told
3	talked	**4**	spoke

(2) ① ② ③ ④

「お母さんが私に部屋をそうじするように言った。」という文にするよ。「(人)に～するように言う」はどう表すかな？
「言う」だけど、say ではないよ。

2 次の(1)と(2)の会話について、(　　)に入れるのに最も適切なものを 1、2、3、4 の中から一つ選び、その番号のマーク欄をぬりつぶしましょう。(10点×2)

(1) ***Sister :*** Let's go to the park and play soccer.

Brother : (　　　) Dad told me to do my homework.

1 Yes, let's.
2 Thanks, I like soccer.
3 Sorry, I'm busy.
4 No, we don't have to.

(1) ① ② ③ ④

(2) ***Mother :*** Your music festival is next Friday.

Son : Yes. I'll call Grandma. (　　　)

1 I want her to come.
2 I can play the piano.
3 She has dance lessons.
4 She is a good cook.

(2) ① ② ③ ④

3 対話と質問を聞き、その答えとして最も適切なものを 1、2、3、4 の中から一つ選びましょう。(5点×2)

♪ 10

(1)
1 Come to the library.
2 Make a test.
3 Play with him.
4 Teach him English.

(1) ① ② ③ ④

(2)
1 Call her back.
2 Talk to her father.
3 Buy some oranges.
4 Take Mike to the store.

(2) ① ② ③ ④

05 英検3級でよく出る単語①
基本の動詞

月　日

点

♪11

★音声を聞き、声に出して読みながらなぞりましょう。

過 …「～した」を表す形

過分 …「～される」と言うときなどに使う形（過去分詞）

（20点）

建てる	閉める、閉まる	持ってくる
build	close	bring
過 過分 built	過 過分 closed	過 過分 brought

加わる、参加する	勝つ	負ける、失う
join	win	lose
過 過分 joined	過 過分 won	過 過分 lost

育てる、育つ	貸す	借りる
grow	lend	borrow
過 grew 過分 grown	過 過分 lent	過 過分 borrowed

救う、節約する	保つ、とっておく	（お金を）使う、（時を）過ごす
save	keep	spend
過 過分 saved	過 過分 kept	過 過分 spent

1 次の(1)と(2)の（　　）に入れるのに最も適切なものを1、2、3、4の中から一つ選び、その番号のマーク欄をぬりつぶしましょう。（10点×2）

(1) Masato started going to high school in April.
He likes music, so he (　　　) the school band.

1 grew　**2** saved
3 held　**4** joined

(1) ① ② ③ ④

(2) ***A:*** Mom, I'm going to go shopping with Ann tomorrow.
B: OK, but don't (　　　) too much money.
You just bought a new skirt last week.

1 spend　**2** rise
3 happen　**4** build

(2) ① ② ③ ④

2 イラストを参考にしながら対話と応答を聞き、最も適切な応答を1、2、3の中から一つ選びましょう。（5点×2）

♪ 12

(1)

(1) ① ② ③

(2)

(2) ① ② ③

06 500年前に建てられたよ
was built など

月　日
点

★音声を聞き、声に出して読みながらなぞりましょう。(10点)

♪13

このお寺はとても古そうだね。
This temple looks very old.

それは500年前に建てられたよ。
It was built 500 years ago.

「～されている」は am/are/is の後に過去分詞（動詞の形の1つ）を続けます。「～された」は was/were の後に過去分詞を続けます。たずねる文は、am/are/is/was/were で文を始めます。

1 次の(1)と(2)の（　　）に入れるのに最も適切なものを 1、2、3、4 の中から一つ選び、その番号のマーク欄をぬりつぶしましょう。(5点×2)

(1) This book is (　　　) in English.

1 write　　2 writing
3 wrote　　4 written

(1) ① ② ③ ④

「英語で書かれています」と表すよ。

(2) Was this picture (　　　) by Picasso?
～によって

1 paints　　2 to paint
3 painted　　4 painting

(2) ① ② ③ ④

「この絵はピカソによってかかれたのですか。」という文にするよ。「かかれた」はどう表すかな？

2 次の（　　）に入れるのに最も適切なものを1、2、3、4の中から一つ選び、その番号のマーク欄をぬりつぶしましょう。(10点)

A **:** Is this singer famous?

B **:** Yes. He's (　　　) all over the country.

1 know　　**2** known
3 knows　　**4** knew

①②③④

3 次の会話について、（　　）に入れるのに最も適切なものを1、2、3、4の中から一つ選び、その番号のマーク欄をぬりつぶしましょう。(10点)

Man **:** Julia, this is a Japanese dish.
It's called *gyu-don*.

Woman **:** (　　　) I saw it on the Internet.

1 Oh, I know that name.
2 I called him, too.
3 I can't speak Japanese.
4 Well, I like cooking.

①②③④

4 対話と質問を聞き、その答えとして最も適切なものを1、2、3、4の中から一つ選びましょう。(5点×2)

♪ 14

(1) **1** 5 years old.　　**2** 15 years old.
3 20 years old.　　**4** 120 years old.

(1) ①②③④

(2) **1** She doesn't like the present.
2 She couldn't take the bus.
3 Her bike was stolen.
4 Her parents are sick.

(2) ①②③④

07 もう宿題を終えたよ
I've already finished ～. など

月　日
点

★音声を聞き、声に出して読みながらなぞりましょう。(10点)

♪15

ぼくはもう宿題を終えたよ。
I've already finished my homework.

本当？　私はまだしてない。
Really? I haven't done mine yet.

I've (already) ～ は「私は(もう)～してしまった」、I haven't ～ (yet) は「私は(まだ)～していない」という意味です。I've は I have を短くした形です。どちらも「～」に過去分詞（動詞の形の1つ）を使います。

1 次の(1)と(2)の（　　）に入れるのに最も適切なものを 1、2、3、4 の中から一つ選び、その番号のマーク欄をぬりつぶしましょう。(5点×2)

(1) Kate has already (　　　) home.

1 goes　　2 going
3 gone　　4 went

(1) ① ② ③ ④

「ケイトはもう家に帰ってしまいました。」
という文にするよ。

(2) *A* : Have you (　　　) that movie yet?
B : No, not yet.

1 see　　2 seen
3 to see　　4 saw

(2) ① ② ③ ④

「もう～したか」とたずねる文は have/has で始め、過去分詞を使うよ。
yet は、たずねる文では「もう」、not のある文では「まだ」だよ。

2 次の（　　）に入れるのに最も適切なものを1、2、3、4の中から一つ選び、その番号のマーク欄をぬりつぶしましょう。（10点）

A : We need some fruit for dessert after dinner.

B : I've (　　　) bought some apples.
They are in the basket on the table.

1 later　**2** already
3 still　**4** over

①②③④

3 次の会話について、（　　）に入れるのに最も適切なものを1、2、3、4の中から一つ選び、その番号のマーク欄をぬりつぶしましょう。（10点）

Woman : Have you had lunch yet?

Man : (　　　) I'm very hungry.

1 Of course.　**2** At the café.
3 Oh, I see.　**4** Not yet.

①②③④

4 対話と質問を聞き、その答えとして最も適切なものを1、2、3、4の中から一つ選びましょう。（5点×2）

♪16

(1)
1 The man.
2 The woman.
3 The man's sister.
4 The woman's sister.

(1) ①②③④

(2)
1 The station is crowded.
2 The bus is late.
3 Billy's friend didn't come.
4 Billy has to work hard.

(2) ①②③④

いっぽずつ…
いっぽずつ…。

08 行ったことがあるよ

I've been to ～. など

月　日

点

★音声を聞き、声に出して読みながらなぞりましょう。(10点)

ヨーロッパに行きたいな。

I want to go to Europe.

私は前にイタリアに行ったことがあるよ。

I've been to Italy before.

I've been to ～ は「私は～に行ったことがある」という意味です。I've の後にさまざまな過去分詞（動詞の形の1つ）を続けて、「私は～したことがある」という意味を表すことができます。

1 次の(1)と(2)の（　　）に入れるのに最も適切なものを 1、2、3、4 の中から一つ選び、その番号のマーク欄をぬりつぶしましょう。(5点×2)

(1) I've never (　　　) a dolphin.

1 see　　2 saw

3 seeing　　4 seen

(1)	① ② ③ ④

have[has] never ～で「(一度も)～したことがない」という意味だよ。

(2) Have you ever (　　　) to Canada?

1 been　　2 go

3 went　　4 to go

(2)	① ② ③ ④

「～したことがあるか」とたずねる文は have/has で始めるよ。
「行ったことがある」はどのように表すかな？

2 次の（　　）に入れるのに最も適切なものを 1、2、3、4 の中から一つ選び、その番号のマーク欄をぬりつぶしましょう。（10点）

A : Have you ever tried Korean food?

B : Yes! I've (　　　) it many times.

1	eat	**2**	ate
3	eaten	**4**	eating

①②③④

3 次の会話について、（　　）に入れるのに最も適切なものを 1、2、3、4 の中から一つ選び、その番号のマーク欄をぬりつぶしましょう。（10点）

Boy 1 : My uncle lives in Australia.

Boy 2 : Oh, (　　　) I held a koala at a zoo.

1 I want to visit there someday.
2 I've been there once.
3 I have an uncle, too.
4 I need a passport.

①②③④

4 イラストを参考にしながら対話と応答を聞き、最も適切な応答を 1、2、3 の中から一つ選びましょう。（5点×2）

(1)

(1) ①②③

(2)

(2) ①②③

09 ずっと寒いね
It has been ～. など

月　日
点

★音声を聞き、声に出して読みながらなぞりましょう。(10点)

今週はずっと寒いね。
It has been cold this week.

うん。新しいコートがほしいな。
Yes. I want a new coat.

have[has] been ～ は「ずっと～(な状態)だ」という意味を表します。
have[has] の後にさまざまな過去分詞(動詞の形の1つ)を続けて、「ずっと～している」という意味を表すことができます。

1 次の(1)と(2)の（　　）に入れるのに最も適切なものを 1、2、3、4 の中から一つ選び、その番号のマーク欄をぬりつぶしましょう。(5点×2)

(1) I've (　　　) in this town for three years.（for ～の間）

1 lived　　2 living
3 live　　4 to live

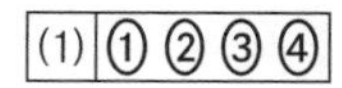

「3年間ずっと住んでいる」という文にするよ。

(2) Ken has (　　　) in his room since this morning.（since ～から(ずっと)）

1 was　　2 is
3 been　　4 be

(2) ① ② ③ ④

「ケンは今朝からずっと自分の部屋にいます。」という文。
「ずっと自分の部屋にいる状態」と考えよう。
「ずっと～な状態だ」はどう表すかな？

2 次の（　　）に入れるのに最も適切なものを 1、2、3、4 の中から一つ選び、その番号のマーク欄をぬりつぶしましょう。（10点）

A : Is Alice your friend?
B : Yes. I've (　　　) her for more than ten years.

1 know　　**2** known
3 knew　　**4** to know

①②③④

3 次の会話について、（　　）に入れるのに最も適切なものを 1、2、3、4 の中から一つ選び、その番号のマーク欄をぬりつぶしましょう。（10点）

Man : Tony looks very tired.
Woman : Yeah. (　　　) He has to finish his work before the vacation.

1 He went to bed early.
2 He's looking for his car key.
3 He has been busy this week.
4 He comes to work by bike.

①②③④

4 英文と質問を聞き、その答えとして最も適切なものを 1、2、3、4 の中から一つ選びましょう。（5点×2）

♪ 20

(1) **1** He had to go to the hospital.
2 He was too tired.
3 He worked with his mother.
4 He has been sick since yesterday.

(1) ①②③④

(2) **1** Her children.　　**2** Her friend.
3 Her students.　　**4** Her aunt.

(2) ①②③④

いっぽずつ…
いっぽずつ…。

10 英検3級でよく出る単語②
基本の動詞・心の中の動きに関する動詞

月　日
点

★音声を聞き、声に出して読みながらなぞりましょう。　♪21

過…「～した」を表す形　（20点）
過分…「～される」と言うときなどに使う形（過去分詞）

招待する
invite
過 過分 invited

しょうかいする
introduce
過 過分 introduced

登る
climb

過 過分 climbed

わたす、合格する、通過する
pass
過 過分 passed

忘れる
forget
過 forgot　過分 forgotten

覚えている、思い出す

remember
過 過分 remembered

のがす、いなくてさびしい
miss
過 過分 missed

決める
decide
過 過分 decided

つかまえる
catch
過 過分 caught

信じる
believe
過 過分 believed

推測する
guess
過 過分 guessed

賛成する
agree
過 過分 agreed

※ forget の過去分詞は forgot の場合もあります。

1 次の(1)と(2)の（　　）に入れるのに最も適切なものを1、2、3、4の中から一つ選び、その番号のマーク欄をぬりつぶしましょう。(10点×2)

(1) A : What did you do last weekend?
B : I (　　　) a mountain with my dad.
The view from the top was great.

1 passed　2 laughed
3 climbed　4 shared

(1) ① ② ③ ④

(2) A : Who is the woman at the door?
B : Well, I think I've seen her somewhere,
but I don't (　　　) her name.

1 follow　2 remember
3 believe　4 raise

(2) ① ② ③ ④

2 対話と質問を聞き、その答えとして最も適切なものを1、2、3、4の中から一つ選びましょう。(5点×2)

♪ 22

(1) 1 Two.　2 Six.
3 Eight.　4 Ten.

(1) ① ② ③ ④

(2) 1 Call his friend.
2 Go fishing.
3 Visit his aunt.
4 Buy a new phone.

(2) ① ② ③ ④

11 ポールと話している子
the child talking with ～ など

月　日
点

★音声を聞き、声に出して読みながらなぞりましょう。(10点)

ポールと話している子はだれ？
Who's the child talking with Paul?

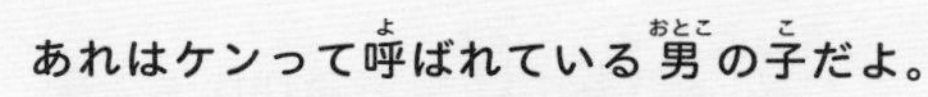

あれはケンって呼ばれている男の子だよ。
That's a boy called Ken.

「～している○○」は、○○の後に〈～ing＋語句〉を続けて表します。「～されている○○」や「～された○○」は、○○の後に〈過去分詞(動詞の形の1つ)＋語句〉を続けて表します。

1 次の(1)と(2)の(　　)に入れるのに最も適切なものを 1、2、3、4 の中から一つ選び、その番号のマーク欄をぬりつぶしましょう。(5点×2)

(1) The girl (　　　) the piano is Kana.

1 play　　**2** plays
3 playing　　**4** played

(1) ① ② ③ ④

「ピアノをひいている少女」と表すよ。

(2) This is a picture (　　　) in London.
(picture: 写真)

1 took　　**2** taking
3 takes　　**4** taken

(2) ① ② ③ ④

前の言葉を説明する語を選ぶときは、「～している」なのか「～されている[された]」なのかを考えよう。

2 次の（　　）に入れるのに最も適切なものを1、2、3、4の中から一つ選び、その番号のマーク欄をぬりつぶしましょう。（10点）

A : What did you do last night?

B : I read a book (　　　) by my favorite singer.

1 write　**2** writing
3 wrote　**4** written

①②③④

3 次の会話について、（　　）に入れるのに最も適切なものを1、2、3、4の中から一つ選び、その番号のマーク欄をぬりつぶしましょう。（10点）

Girl : Look at that woman.

Boy : Which woman?

Girl : (　　　) It looks great on her.

1 She's my history teacher.
2 The one wearing a blue dress.
3 The tallest one.
4 This is her birthday party.

①②③④

4 対話と質問を聞き、その答えとして最も適切なものを1、2、3、4の中から一つ選びましょう。（5点×2）

♪ 24

(1) **1** By the door.　**2** In the science room.
3 At the gate.　**4** In the supermarket.

(1) ①②③④

(2) **1** He went to Japan.
2 He worked hard.
3 He bought a car.
4 He cooked lunch.

(2) ①②③④

12 パリに住むおば
an aunt who lives in ～ など

月　日
点

★音声を聞き、声に出して読みながらなぞりましょう。(10点)

ぼくにはパリに住むおばさんがいるよ。
I have an aunt who lives in Paris.

わ、それって私がおとずれたい街だよ。
Oh, that's the city I want to visit.

who や that で始まるまとまりを「人」の後に続けて、「人」を説明することができます。「もの」の場合は which か that を使います。後にくる説明が「○○が～する」という意味の場合は、who、which、that は省略できます。

1 次の(1)と(2)の（　）に入れるのに最も適切なものを 1、2、3、4 の中から一つ選び、その番号のマーク欄をぬりつぶしましょう。(5点×2)

(1) I know a boy (　　　) speaks Chinese.

1 which　**2** when
3 where　**4** who

(1) ① ② ③ ④

boy は「人」だね。「中国語を話す男の子」と表すよ。

(2) This is a café (　　　) is popular among young girls.
～の間で人気がある

1 which　**2** when
3 where　**4** who

(2) ① ② ③ ④

café は「もの」だね。「ここは若い少女たちの間で人気のカフェです。」という文だよ。

2 次の（　　）に入れるのに最も適切なものを1、2、3、4の中から一つ選び、その番号のマーク欄をぬりつぶしましょう。（10点）

A : I want to see the pictures (　　　) you took in Okinawa.

B : OK. I'll bring them tomorrow.

1 this　　**2** that

3 it　　**4** these

①②③④

3 次の会話について、（　　）に入れるのに最も適切なものを1、2、3、4の中から一つ選び、その番号のマーク欄をぬりつぶしましょう。（10点）

Boy : I heard Ms. Green sang in her class.

Girl : Yes. (　　　) so I was happy.

1 She's an English teacher,

2 She was in the music room,

3 She sang a song I like very much,

4 She has a dog that can swim well,

①②③④

4 対話と質問を聞き、その答えとして最も適切なものを1、2、3、4の中から一つ選びましょう。（5点×2）

♪ 26

(1) **1** At an airport.　　**2** At a restaurant.

3 At a bookstore.　　**4** At a station.

(1) ①②③④

(2) **1** She has to return it tomorrow.

2 It's her homework.

3 She's interested in Egypt.

4 Her friend lent it to her.

(2) ①②③④

13 ニックネームを教えて

tell me ～ / call me ～ など

月　日

点

★音声を聞き、声に出して読みながらなぞりましょう。（10点）

あなたのニックネームを教えて。

Please tell me your nickname.

友達は私をメグって呼ぶよ。

My friends call me Meg.

tell A B で「A に B を伝える、教える」という意味です。give（あたえる）、show（見せる）、lend（貸す）なども同じ形で使えます。call A B は「A を B と呼ぶ」。同じ形の make A B は「A を B にする」という意味です。

1 次の(1)と(2)の（　　）に入れるのに最も適切なものを 1、2、3、4 の中から一つ選び、その番号のマーク欄をぬりつぶしましょう。（5点×2）

(1) Can you (　　　) me your notebook?（notebook：ノート）

1 see　　2 look
3 show　　4 watch

(1) ① ② ③ ④

「私にあなたのノートを見せてくれる？」
という文にするよ。

(2) The news (　　　) me sad.（news：知らせ、sad：悲しい）

1 made　　2 called
3 gave　　4 took

(2) ① ② ③ ④

「その知らせは私を悲しくさせました。」という文だよ。
「A を B にする」はどう表すかな？

2 次の（　　）に入れるのに最も適切なものを1、2、3、4の中から一つ選び、その番号のマーク欄をぬりつぶしましょう。（10点）

A : Can you (　　　) me your red pen? I forgot mine.

B : Sure. Here you are.

1 borrow　　**2** lend
3 put　　**4** tell

①②③④

3 次の会話について、（　　）に入れるのに最も適切なものを1、2、3、4の中から一つ選び、その番号のマーク欄をぬりつぶしましょう。（10点）

Boy : Look. I took a nice picture. (　　　)

Girl : Oh, beautiful! That'll make her happy.

1 I want a new camera.
2 My sister often goes to museums.
3 I'll send it to Lisa by e-mail.
4 Ms. Brown told me the news.

①②③④

4 イラストを参考にしながら対話と応答を聞き、最も適切な応答を1、2、3の中から一つ選びましょう。（5点×2）

(1)

(1) ①②③

(2)

(2) ①②③

14 何なのか知ってる？

what this is / ～, isn't it? など

月　日
点

★音声を聞き、声に出して読みながらなぞりましょう。（10点）

これが何なのか知ってる？

Do you know what this is?

おもちゃだよね？

It's a toy, isn't it?

「これは何？」は What is this? ですが、Do you know ～? などの別の文に入ると what this is の語順になります。また、It's ～. の文で「～ですよね。」と確かめたり同意を求めたりするときは、文の最後に “, isn't it?” をつけます。

1 次の(1)と(2)の（　　）に入れるのに最も適切なものを 1、2、3、4 の中から一つ選び、その番号のマーク欄をぬりつぶしましょう。（5点×2）

(1) I don't know (　　　) Emma lives.

1 what　　2 where
3 when　　4 who

(1) ① ② ③ ④

エマが住んでいるところを知らないんだね。

(2) You have a dog, (　　　) you?

1 aren't　　2 don't
3 isn't　　4 didn't

(2) ① ② ③ ④

「あなたはイヌを飼っていますよね。」という文だよ。「あなたはイヌを飼っていますか。」とたずねるときに使う語がヒントだよ。

2 次の（　　）に入れるのに最も適切なものを1、2、3、4の中から一つ選び、その番号のマーク欄をぬりつぶしましょう。（10点）

A : Please tell me (　　　) Peter will come to Osaka.

B : He'll come on July 7. I'm going to meet him at the airport.

1 when　**2** where
3 why　**4** how

①②③④

3 次の会話について、（　　）に入れるのに最も適切なものを1、2、3、4の中から一つ選び、その番号のマーク欄をぬりつぶしましょう。（10点）

Brother : Grandpa's birthday is coming soon, isn't it?

Sister : Yes, it's next week. Let's buy a present for him. (　　　)

1 I don't know when it is.
2 He had a party.
3 I know what he wants.
4 He likes shopping.

①②③④

4 対話と質問を聞き、その答えとして最も適切なものを1、2、3、4の中から一つ選びましょう。（5点×2）

♪ 30

(1) **1** In the gym.　**2** By the entrance.
3 In a sports shop.　**4** Outside.

(1) ①②③④

(2) **1** She bought a train ticket.
2 She saw a musical.
3 She enjoyed shopping.
4 She watched a baseball game.

(2) ①②③④

あと
ちょっとで
はんぶんだ…!!!

15 英検3級でよく出る単語③
身の回りのもの・人

月　日　点

★音声を聞き、声に出して読みながらなぞりましょう。
(20点)

服

clothes

さいふ

wallet

切手

stamp

鏡

mirror

ごみ

garbage

せん風機、うちわ、ファン

fan

作家

writer

宇宙飛行士

astronaut

シェフ、料理人

chef

芸術家

artist

夫

husband

妻

wife

1 次の(1)と(2)の（　　）に入れるのに最も適切なものを1、2、3、4の中から一つ選び、その番号のマーク欄をぬりつぶしましょう。(10点×2)

(1) **A:** I like books. I want to write stories for children in the future.

B: So you want to be a (　　　). Nice dream!

1 chef　　2 engineer
3 designer　　4 writer

(1) ①②③④

(2) **A:** Maria, something is on your face. Look in the (　　　).

B: Oh, it's my dog's hair. Thank you.

1 blanket　　2 wallet
3 mirror　　4 scissors

(2) ①②③④

2 英文と質問を聞き、その答えとして最も適切なものを1、2、3、4の中から一つ選びましょう。(5点×2)

♪ 32

(1) 1 Two.　　2 Three.
3 Seven.　　4 Ten.

(1) ①②③④

(2) 1 The man.
2 The man's wife.
3 The man's friend.
4 The man's brother.

(2) ①②③④

16 400メートル泳げたよ
be able to ～ など

月　日
点

★音声を聞き、声に出して読みながらなぞりましょう。（10点）

400メートル泳げたよ。
I was able to swim 400 meters.

すごい！　あなたをほこりに思うわ。
Great! I'm proud of you.

be able to ～ は「～することができる」という意味です。be proud of ～ は「～をほこりに思う」という意味です。「be」は、ふつう am/are/is/was/were を使います。will や can の後では be です。

1 次の(1)と(2)の（　　）に入れるのに最も適切なものを 1、2、3、4 の中から一つ選び、その番号のマーク欄をぬりつぶしましょう。（5点×2）

(1) Don't be (　　　) for school.

1	slow	**2**	late
3	rich	**4**	same

(1) ① ② ③ ④

「学校におくれてはいけません。」という文だよ。
「おくれた」を表す語を使うよ。

(2) The music room was (　　　) of students.

1	loud	**2**	wrong
3	wild	**4**	full

(2) ① ② ③ ④

「音楽室は生徒でいっぱいでした。」という文だよ。
「いっぱいの」を表す語は…？

2 次の（　　）に入れるのに最も適切なものを1、2、3、4の中から一つ選び、その番号のマーク欄をぬりつぶしましょう。（10点）

A : It's dark outside.

B : Yeah. The sky is (　　　) with clouds.

1 covered　　**2** bright

3 useful　　**4** clever

①②③④

3 次の会話について、（　　）に入れるのに最も適切なものを1、2、3、4の中から一つ選び、その番号のマーク欄をぬりつぶしましょう。（10点）

Woman : (　　　) Ted?

Man : Of course. I've already finished the sales report.

1 Have you worked here for many years,

2 Are you ready for the meeting,

3 Do you go to work by bike,

4 Were you tired of business trips,

①②③④

4 対話と質問を聞き、その答えとして最も適切なものを1、2、3、4の中から一つ選びましょう。（5点×2）

(1) **1** Bread.　　**2** Sandwiches.

3 Curry and rice.　　**4** Pizza.

(1) ①②③④

(2) **1** He talked with his friend.

2 He cleaned the hall.

3 He went to a concert.

4 He helped some people.

(2) ①②③④

17 映画に行かない？

Why don't we ～? など

月　日
点

♪ 35

★音声を聞き、声に出して読みながらなぞりましょう。（10点）

映画に行かない？
Why don't we go to a movie?

いいね。
That sounds great.

Why don't we ～? は「（いっしょに）～しませんか。」という意味です。That sounds great.（いいですね。）は That を省略することもあります。(That's a) good idea.（いい考えですね。）などの応答もあります。

1 次の(1)と(2)の（　　）に入れるのに最も適切なものを 1、2、3、4 の中から一つ選び、その番号のマーク欄をぬりつぶしましょう。（5点×2）

(1) ***A*** **:** (　　　) about having a party for Jim?
B **:** Sounds like fun.

1 Which　　**2** When
3 How　　**4** Where

(1) ① ② ③ ④

(2) ***A*** **:** (　　　) you like to come to my house for dinner?
B **:** Sure. Thank you.

1 Can　　**2** Would
3 Could　　**4** Shall

(2) ① ② ③ ④

Do you want to ～? のていねいな言い方で、「～しませんか。」と誘っているよ。like の後に、to ～ ではなく食べ物などを続けると、「～はどうですか。」とすすめる言い方になるよ。

2 次の(1)と(2)の会話について、(　　)に入れるのに最も適切なものを 1、2、3、4 の中から一つ選び、その番号のマーク欄をぬりつぶしましょう。(10点×2)

(1) ***Boy :*** Do you want to play tennis with me tomorrow?

Girl : (　　　) I'll bring my racket.

1 No, thank you.
2 Yes, I want some.
3 You did a great job.
4 I'd love to.

(1) ① ② ③ ④

(2) ***Woman 1 :*** Shall we go shopping this weekend?

Woman 2 : Sorry, I'm busy. (　　　)

1 Maybe some other time.
2 I'd like some coffee.
3 Same to you.
4 That's a good idea.

(2) ① ② ③ ④

3 イラストを参考にしながら対話と応答を聞き、最も適切な応答を 1、2、3 の中から一つ選びましょう。(5点×2)

♪ 36

(1)

(1) ① ② ③

(2)

(2) ① ② ③

いいにおいがしてきたよ!!

18 試着してもいいですか？

May I try on ～? など

月　日

点

♪ 37

★音声を聞き、声に出して読みながらなぞりましょう。（10点）

このコートを試着してもいいですか。

May I try on this coat?

もちろんです。鏡はあちらにあります。

Sure. The mirror is over there.

May[Can] I try on ～? は「～を試着してもいいですか。」という意味です。try ～ on の語順の場合もあります。応答は Please come this way.（こちらへどうぞ。）などもあります。

1 次の(1)と(2)の（　　）に入れるのに最も適切なものを 1、2、3、4 の中から一つ選び、その番号のマーク欄をぬりつぶしましょう。（5点×2）

売り切れだと言っているよ。

(1) ***A :*** I'm looking for the new book by Julia White.

B : Sorry, it's (　　　) out.

1 made　　**2** written

3 held　　**4** sold

(1) ① ② ③ ④

(2) ***A :*** May I take your (　　　)?

B : Yes. I'd like steak with salad, please.

ステーキ

1 order　　**2** knife

3 memory　　**4** price

(2) ① ② ③ ④

注文をたずねているよ。「注文」「注文する」という意味の語を入れよう。応答の I'd like ～. は I want ～. のていねいな言い方だよ。

2 次の(1)と(2)の会話について、(　　)に入れるのに最も適切なものを 1、2、3、4 の中から一つ選び、その番号のマーク欄をぬりつぶしましょう。(10点×2)

(1) ***Man :*** This jacket is nice. (　　　)
Salesclerk : Certainly. Please come this way.

1 How much is it?
2 Can I try it on?
3 Do you have a jacket?
4 How about that one?

(1) ① ② ③ ④

(2) ***Woman :*** Can I have seafood spaghetti, please?
Waiter : Sure. (　　　)
Woman : No, that's all.

1 Why not?
2 Shall I call you?
3 Anything else?
4 Are you sure?

(2) ① ② ③ ④

3 対話と質問を聞き、その答えとして最も適切なものを 1、2、3、4 の中から一つ選びましょう。(5点×2)

♪ 38

(1)
1 A black cap.　　2 A black shirt.
3 A blue cap.　　4 A blue shirt.

(1) ① ② ③ ④

(2)
1 At an art museum.
2 At a restaurant.
3 At a post office.
4 At a supermarket.

(2) ① ② ③ ④

19 病院はありますか？

Is there ～? / Go down ～. など

月　日

点

♪39

★音声を聞き、声に出して読みながらなぞりましょう。(10点)

この近くに病院はありますか。

Is there a hospital near here?

はい。この通りを行ってください。

Yes. Go down this street.

Is there ～? は「～はありますか。」という意味です。道・行き方をたずねるときは、Can you tell me ～?（私に～を教えてくれますか。）などもよく使います。go down ～ は「（道などにそって）行く」という意味です。

1 次の(1)と(2)の（　　）に入れるのに最も適切なものを 1、2、3、4 の中から一つ選び、その番号のマーク欄をぬりつぶしましょう。(5点×2)

「まっすぐ行って、2つ目の角で左に曲がる」と言っているよ。

(1) ***A :*** Is there a post office around here?

B : Yes. Go (　　　) and turn left at the second corner.

（turn：曲がる　corner：角）

1 greatly　**2** straight

3 suddenly　**4** almost

(1)	① ② ③ ④

(2) ***A :*** Can you tell me (　　　) City Hall is?

B : Sure. It's on the next block.

（City Hall：市役所　block：ブロック）

1 what　**2** when

3 where　**4** which

(2)	① ② ③ ④

市役所について何を教えてほしいのかな？　Bは「それはとなりのブロックにあります。」と言っているよ。

2 次の(1)と(2)の会話について、(　　)に入れるのに最も適切なものを 1、2、3、4 の中から一つ選び、その番号のマーク欄をぬりつぶしましょう。(10点×2)

(1) ***Girl :*** I'd like to go to the science museum. (　　　)
Boy : Take the train to Park Station.

1 What can I see there?
2 Would you like to come?
3 Where's your textbook?
4 How can I get there?

(1) ① ② ③ ④

(2) ***Man :*** Excuse me. Could you tell me the way to the stadium?
Woman : I'm sorry, but I don't know. (　　　)

1 I can't play baseball.
2 I'm not from here.
3 It was built last year.
4 That's kind of you.

(2) ① ② ③ ④

3 イラストを参考にしながら対話と応答を聞き、最も適切な応答を 1、2、3 の中から一つ選びましょう。(5点×2)

♪ 40

(1)

(1) ① ② ③

(2)

(2) ① ② ③

英検３級でよく出る単語④
施設など・形のないもの

月　日
点

♪ 41

★音声を聞き、声に出して読みながらなぞりましょう。
（20点）

庭
garden

大学
college

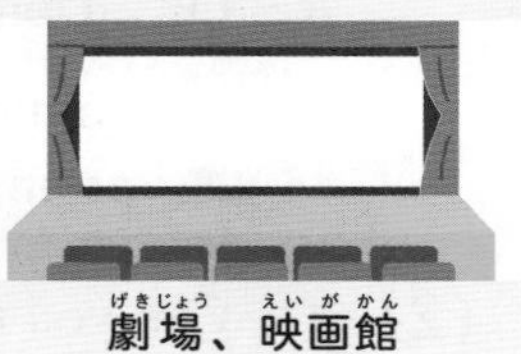

劇場、映画館
theater

工場
factory

教会
church

入り口
entrance

伝言、メッセージ
message

情報
information

事故
accident

ちがい
difference

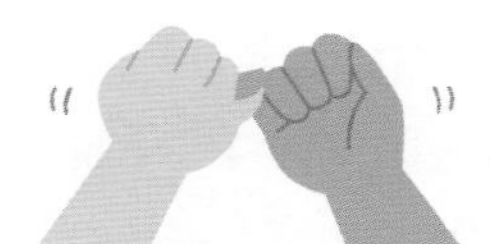

約束
promise

秘密
secret

1 次(つぎ)の(1)と(2)の（　　）に入(い)れるのに最(もっと)も適切(てきせつ)なものを1、2、3、4 の中(なか)から一(ひと)つ選(えら)び、その番号(ばんごう)のマーク欄(らん)をぬりつぶしましょう。（10点(てん)×2）

(1) ***A :*** I'll be back by six and do my homework after dinner.

B : OK. Don't break your (　　　).

1 opinion　　**2** secret
3 promise　　**4** reason

(1) ① ② ③ ④

(2) ***A :*** Can you tell me how to get to the (　　　)?

B : Sure. Go down this street for two blocks. It's on your left.

1 theater　　**2** accident
3 schedule　　**4** language

(2) ① ② ③ ④

2 対話(たいわ)と質問(しつもん)を聞(き)き、その答(こた)えとして最(もっと)も適切(てきせつ)なものを1、2、3、4 の中(なか)から一(ひと)つ選(えら)びましょう。（5点(てん)×2）

♪ 42

(1) **1** She went to a college.
2 She took an art class.
3 She enjoyed pizza.
4 She visited a church.

(1) ① ② ③ ④

(2) **1** To play games.
2 To read the news.
3 To get information.
4 To help his mother.

(2) ① ② ③ ④

21 ポールをお願いできますか？
May I speak to ～? など

月　日
点

★音声を聞き、声に出して読みながらなぞりましょう。（10点）

♪43

ポールをお願いできますか。
May I speak to Paul?

わかった。少し待ってね。
OK. Just a moment.

電話をかけるときは、May I speak to ～?（～をお願いできますか。）や Is ～ home?（～はいますか。）などと言います。応答は Sorry, he's out now.（すみません、彼は今、外出中です。）などもあります。

1 次の(1)と(2)の（　　）に入れるのに最も適切なものを 1、2、3、4 の中から一つ選び、その番号のマーク欄をぬりつぶしましょう。（5点×2）

「（電話を切らずに）待ってください。」という表現だよ。

(1) ***A*:** Hello, this is Kate. Is Robert home?
***B*:** Hi, Kate. (　　　) on, please.

1 Hold　**2** Speak
3 Pick　**4** Hurry

(1) ① ② ③ ④

(2) ***A*:** Can I speak to Manami, please?
***B*:** Sorry, she's out now. Do you want to leave a (　　　)?

leave：残す

1 chance　**2** message
3 meaning　**4** trouble

(2) ① ② ③ ④

電話をかけた相手がいなかったんだね。「～を残したいですか。」と聞かれているよ。こんなとき、何を残したいかな？

2 次の(1)と(2)の会話について、(　　)に入れるのに最も適切なものを 1、2、3、4 の中から一つ選び、その番号のマーク欄をぬりつぶしましょう。(10点×2)

(1) ***Man :*** Hello. May I speak to Mr. Harris?
Woman : Sure. (　　　)

1 Good job.　　2 Have a nice day.
3 I'm OK.　　4 Just a minute, please.

(1) ① ② ③ ④

(2) ***Girl :*** Hello. Is Mike home?
Man : Sorry, he went to the library.
Can I take a message?
Girl : No, thank you. (　　　)

1 I don't like books.
2 I'll call back later.
3 Let me see.
4 That sounds good.

(2) ① ② ③ ④

3 対話と質問を聞き、その答えとして最も適切なものを 1、2、3、4 の中から一つ選びましょう。(5点×2)

♪ 44

(1)
1 Meet at the station.
2 Visit their coach.
3 Play soccer.
4 Run in the park.

(1) ① ② ③ ④

(2)
1 Have lunch with him.
2 Call him back.
3 Give him a message.
4 Speak in Japanese.

(2) ① ② ③ ④

意見を書く 英作文①

月　日
点

1 ライティング（25点）

- あなたは、外国人の友達から以下のQUESTIONをされました。
- QUESTIONについて、あなたの考えとその理由を2つ英文で書きなさい。
- 語数の目安は25語～35語です。
- 解答は、以下の解答欄に書きなさい。
- 解答がQUESTIONに対応していないと判断された場合は、0点と採点されることがあります。QUESTIONをよく読んでから答えてください。

QUESTION
What do you like to do in your free time?

1つ目の理由（2文目）は、This is because ～.（これは～だからです。）の形で書こう。2つ目の理由（3文目）は、Also,（また、）に続けて書こう。

1文目：自分の意見を書こう

2文目：1つ目の理由を書こう

3文目：2つ目の理由を書こう

最後に：語数を確認しよう

2 ライティング（25点）

- あなたは、外国人の友達から以下のQUESTIONをされました。
- QUESTIONについて、あなたの考えとその理由を2つ英文で書きなさい。
- 語数の目安は25語～35語です。
- 解答は、以下の解答欄に書きなさい。
- 解答がQUESTIONに対応していないと判断された場合は、0点と採点されることがあります。QUESTIONをよく読んでから答えてください。

QUESTION

Which do you like better, going to the mountains or going to the beach?

23 Eメールへの返信を書く①
英作文②

月　日
点

ライティング（50点）

- あなたは、外国人の友達(Lisa)から以下のEメールを受け取りました。Eメールを読み、それに対する返信メールを、□に英文で書きなさい。
- あなたが書く返信メールの中で、友達（Lisa）からの2つの質問（下線部）に対応する内容を、あなた自身で自由に考えて答えなさい。
- あなたが書く返信メールの中で□に書く英文の語数の目安は、15語～25語です。
- 解答は、次のページの解答欄に書きなさい。
- 解答が友達（Lisa）のEメールに対応していないと判断された場合は、0点と採点されることがあります。友達（Lisa）のEメールをよく読んでから答えてください。
- □の下のBest wishes, の後にあなたの名前を書く必要はありません。

> Hi,
>
> Thank you for your e-mail.
> I heard you went camping with your family. I want to know more about it. How was the weather? And what did you enjoy the most?
>
> Your friend,
> Lisa

① How was the weather?（天気はどうでしたか。）と、② What did you enjoy the most?（何を最も楽しみましたか。）の2つの質問に答えよう。

Hi, Lisa!

Thank you for your e-mail.

解答欄(かいとうらん)に記入(きにゅう)しなさい。

Best wishes,

【解答欄(かいとうらん)】

24 Eメールへの返信を書く②
英作文③

月　日
点

ライティング（50点）

- あなたは、外国人の友達（Greg）から以下のEメールを受け取りました。Eメールを読み、それに対する返信メールを、□に英文で書きなさい。
- あなたが書く返信メールの中で、友達（Greg）からの2つの質問（下線部）に対応する内容を、あなた自身で自由に考えて答えなさい。
- あなたが書く返信メールの中で□に書く英文の語数の目安は、15語～25語です。
- 解答は、次のページの解答欄に書きなさい。
- 解答が友達（Greg）のEメールに対応していないと判断された場合は、<u>0点と採点されることがあります。</u>友達（Greg）のEメールをよく読んでから答えてください。
- □の下のBest wishes, の後にあなたの名前を書く必要はありません。

> Hi,
>
> Thank you for your e-mail.
> You visited your grandparents during the vacation, right? I want to know more about it. <u>How long did you stay at their house? And what did you do with them?</u>
>
> Your friend,
> Greg

① How long did you stay at their house?（どれくらい彼ら（＝祖父母）の家にとまりましたか。）と、② What did you do with them?（彼らと何をしましたか。）の2つの質問に答えよう。

Hi, Greg!

Thank you for your e-mail.

解答欄(かいとうらん)に記入(きにゅう)しなさい。

Best wishes,

【解答欄(かいとうらん)】

25 英検3級でよく出る単語⑤
様子・感情を表す言葉など

月　日
点

♪ 45

★音声を聞き、声に出して読みながらなぞりましょう。
（20点）

おこって	こわがって	うれしい
angry	afraid	glad

おどろいて	きんちょうして	はずかしがりの
surprised	nervous	shy

高価な	十分な、十分に	よごれた
expensive	enough	dirty
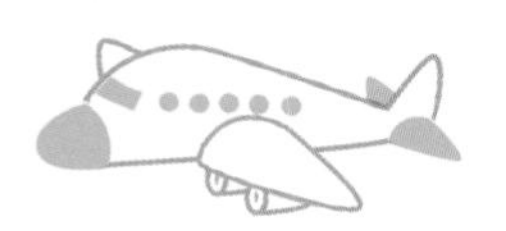		
外国に、外国で	はっきりと	ひとりで
abroad	clearly	alone

1 次の(1)と(2)の(　　)に入れるのに最も適切なものを1、2、3、4 の中から一つ選び、その番号のマーク欄をぬりつぶしましょう。(10点×2)

(1) **A :** In my class, try to speak English a lot.
Don't be (　　　) of making mistakes.
B : OK, Mr. Miller. I will try.

1 surprised　**2** afraid
3 excited　**4** relaxed

(1) ① ② ③ ④

(2) **A :** What do you want to do in the future?
B : I want to study (　　　).
I'm interested in other cultures.

1 recently　**2** clearly
3 almost　**4** abroad

(2) ① ② ③ ④

2 イラストを参考にしながら対話と応答を聞き、最も適切な応答を 1、2、3 の中から一つ選びましょう。(5点×2)

♪ 46

(1)

(1) ① ② ③

(2)

(2) ① ② ③

26 掲示・案内 長文問題①

1 次の掲示の内容に関して、(1)と(2)の質問に対する答えとして最も適切なもの、または文を完成させるのに最も適切なものを 1、2、3、4 の中から一つ選び、その番号のマーク欄をぬりつぶしましょう。(10点×2)

Let's have a party!

Christmas season has come. That means (〜を意味する) it's time for the cooking club's Christmas party! The members will make cakes, cookies, and some snacks (軽食) to have a great time with you. Why don't you come?

When : December 20 from 3:30 p.m. to 5:30 p.m.

Where : School Cafeteria

Students who want to come to the party have to visit the cooking room to sign up ((参加)申しこみをする) by December 17. We need some people who can set the tables with us on the day. If you can be a volunteer, please talk to Ms. Baker.

At the party, Mr. Grant, our music teacher, will play some Christmas songs on the piano. Let's enjoy singing together!

パーティーのために、料理部の部員は何をすると書いてあるかな？

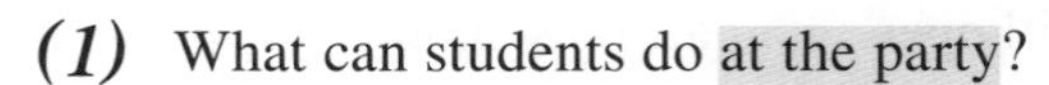

(1) What can students do at the party?

1 Play the piano.　2 Bake a Christmas cake.
3 Eat some snacks.　4 Join the music club.

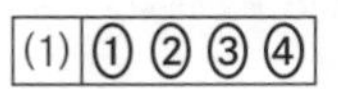

(1) ① ② ③ ④

(2) If students can help the club members, they have to

1 sing with Mr. Grant.
2 join a volunteer group.
3 talk to Ms. Baker.
4 clean the cooking room.

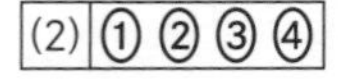

(2) ① ② ③ ④

2 次の掲示の内容に関して、(1)と(2)の質問に対する答えとして最も適切なもの、または文を完成させるのに最も適切なものを 1、2、3、4 の中から一つ選び、その番号のマーク欄をぬりつぶしましょう。(15点×2)

A New Shop in the Clayton Art Museum

A new gift shop will open in the Clayton Art Museum on July 2. There will be a lot of original goods. You can find nice gifts for your family, friends, or yourself such as T-shirts, cups, and shopping bags.

Opening Hours : Weekdays 10 a.m. to 7 p.m. (On Mondays, closed)
Weekends 9:30 a.m. to 7:30 p.m.

If you spend over 50 dollars, you will get a set of special postcards. They have beautiful pictures of the museum on them.

We will have an opening sale for one week(July 2-8). All items will be sold for 10% off. Enjoy shopping before or after you enjoy our great works of art.

(1) What is this notice about?

1 A special cup that will be shown in July.
2 An art museum that has pictures of families.
3 A gift given to a famous artist.
4 A shop that will open in an art museum.

(1) ① ② ③ ④

(2) People who spend over 50 dollars at the shop will receive

1 an original cup.
2 a set of postcards.
3 a 10% off ticket.
4 a free T-shirt.

(2) ① ② ③ ④

27 Eメール 長文問題②

月　日　点

1 次のEメールの内容に関して、(1)と(2)の質問に対する答えとして最も適切なものを 1、2、3、4 の中から一つ選び、その番号のマーク欄をぬりつぶしましょう。(10点×2)

From: Alison Price
To: Josh Morgan
Date: May 11
Subject: Ms. Lopez

Hi Josh,

I heard sad news about Ms. Lopez. She's going to go back to her country next month. Did you know that? David told me the news today. He said he was sad, too. Her Spanish class is a lot of fun, and I also enjoyed dancing with her at the school festival. I want to do something for her. How about having a party? We have a few weeks to prepare, so we can do something special. What do you think?

Your friend,

Alison

スペイン語の

準備をする

メールの "go back" を問題では "return" に言いかえているよ。

(1) When will Ms. Lopez return to her country?

1 In May.　　2 Next month.
3 In a week.　　4 Today.

(1) ① ② ③ ④

(2) What does Alison want to do?

1 Tell David about Ms. Lopez.
2 Dance at the school festival.
3 Give something special to Josh.
4 Have a party for Ms. Lopez.

(2) ① ② ③ ④

2 次のEメール（**1**への返信）の内容に関して、（1）と（2）の質問に対する答えとして最も適切なもの、または文を完成させるのに最も適切なものを1、2、3、4の中から一つ選び、その番号のマーク欄をぬりつぶしましょう。

（15点×2）

> From: Josh Morgan
> To: Alison Price
> Date: May 11
> Subject: Good idea
>
> ---
>
> Hey Alison,
> I'm surprised to hear the news. I like her class, too, so I'll miss her. Having a party is a good idea! I think we can make a video message. It's easy to shoot* videos with a smartphone. Let's ask students and teachers to give her a message. But I'm not sure that it's OK to use my smartphone at school. I'll ask Mr. Logan tomorrow. Maybe others have different ideas. Why don't we talk with David and other friends after school?
> See you,
> Josh
>
> *shoot：さつえいする

(1) Why is Josh surprised?

1 Alison gave him a video message.
2 He couldn't use his smartphone at school.
3 He didn't know the news.
4 Teachers asked him about the party.

(1) ① ② ③ ④

(2) Tomorrow, Josh will

1 ask Mr. Logan about using his smartphone at school.
2 make a video message with friends.
3 invite David to a party at his house.
4 ask students and teachers about the news.

(2) ① ② ③ ④

説明文（人物について）長文問題③

月　日　点

1 次の英文の内容に関して、(1)と(2)の質問に対する答えとして最も適切なものを 1、2、3、4 の中から一つ選び、その番号のマーク欄をぬりつぶしましょう。(10点×2)

Mary Anderson

Mary Anderson was born in Alabama in 1866. When she was four, her father died. Anderson and her family, her mother and sister, were able to get money from her father's land. In 1893, Anderson moved to California and started a business. She owned a large farm for cows and a field for grapes to make wine. In 1898, Anderson returned to Alabama to help her sick aunt.

In the winter of 1902, Anderson visited New York. When she was on a tram* there, she noticed one thing. It was hard for the driver to see outside because of the snow on the front window. He had to stop the tram, get out, and clean the window with his hands. This gave Anderson an idea to solve a problem for drivers. It was a window cleaning tool, a windshield wiper.*

*tram：路面電車　*windshield wiper：(車の)ワイパー

(1) When did Anderson move to California?

1 In 1866.
2 In 1893.
3 In 1898.
4 In 1902.

"California" を手がかりに、文章を読み返そう。

(1) ① ② ③ ④

(2) Why couldn't the tram driver see outside well?

1 Some people were cleaning the tram.
2 It was dark outside in New York.
3 There was snow on the front window.
4 He had a problem with his eyes.

(2) ① ② ③ ④

2 次の英文(**1**の続き)の内容に関して、(1)と(2)の質問に対する答えとして最も適切なもの、または文を完成させるのに最も適切なものを 1、2、3、4 の中から一つ選び、その番号のマーク欄をぬりつぶしましょう。(15点×2)

After she was back to Alabama, Anderson started to make her windshield wiper. It had a lever* to move a stick with rubber* on it. Drivers could clean the window with the wiper by using the lever from inside the car. Anderson tried to sell her idea, but no companies bought it. They did not think that the wiper was good for them because most people did not have a car.

In 1922, a car maker called Cadillac started to put Anderson's wiper on their cars. Driving was more and more popular at that time, but there was no way to clean the front window on people's cars. Cadillac thought that it was good to use Anderson's idea. The system of her wipers is basically the same as today's wipers. Today drivers can drive safely on rainy or snowy days thanks to Anderson.

*lever：レバー　*rubber：ゴム

(1) Companies didn't buy Andreson's wiper because

1 cars were not popular.
2 it was very expensive.
3 it had a lever for drivers.
4 they had a better idea.

(1) ① ② ③ ④

(2) What happened in 1922?

1 Anderson made a new type of windshield wiper.
2 A car maker began making cars with Anderson's wiper.
3 Anderson started to work at a car company.
4 More people did not drive on rainy days.

(2) ① ② ③ ④

29 説明文（物事について）長文問題④

月　日
点

1 次の英文の内容に関して、(1)と(2)の質問に対する答えとして最も適切なものを 1、2、3、4 の中から一つ選び、その番号のマーク欄をぬりつぶしましょう。(10点×2)

A Miracle* Tree

Neem is a tree from India. It grows fast and becomes about 20 meters tall. Its flower is small and white, and its fruit looks like an olive. Neem is called a miracle tree because all parts of the tree are useful for people. In India, people have used neem trees in many ways for 4,500 years. For example, it is popular to use neem twigs* as toothbrushes.* People can keep their teeth healthy by using these brushes.

People in India think that neem trees are good for health. They can be medicine when you have a fever or when you are sick. So in India, people plant the tree in their yard. Its leaves and other parts are also used in Indian dishes. There is neem leaf tea, too. It tastes bitter.

*miracle：きせきの　*twig：小枝　*toothbrush：歯ブラシ

"neem twigs" を手がかりに文章を読み返そう。

(1) What do people in India do with neem twigs?

1 They eat fruit.
2 They keep their yard clean.
3 They paint pictures.
4 They clean their teeth.

(1) ① ② ③ ④

(2) Why do people plant neem trees in their yard?

1 The fruit tastes like an olive.
2 They can make medicine from the tree.
3 They use them to wash the dishes.
4 The trees grow very quickly.

(2) ① ② ③ ④

2 次の英文（**1**の続き）の内容に関して、(1)と(2)の質問に対する答えとして最も適切なもの、または文を完成させるのに最も適切なものを 1、2、3、4 の中から一つ選び、その番号のマーク欄をぬりつぶしましょう。（15点×2）

Many kinds of insects* do not like neem. In 1959, a very large group of locusts* came to Sudan, and every plant was eaten by them. However, only neem trees were standing on the field after the locusts left. You can use neem leaves or twigs to protect your clothes or food from insects. Also, neem oil is useful for gardening. It protects your plants. You can get the oil from neem fruit and seeds.* The fruit and the seeds after you take the oil are called neem cake. It is good to put neem cake on the ground in your garden. Your plants will grow well.

There are also other ways to use neem, such as neem soap or neem shampoo. Neem has a lot of good points, so scientists study it in many parts of the world.

*insect：こん虫　*locust：イナゴ　*seed：種

(1) We can use neem oil to

1 make clothes for gardening.
2 protect our plants from insects.
3 catch a group of locusts.
4 bake a special cake.

(1) ①②③④

(2) What is this story about?

1 Medicine used for a fever in India.
2 Oil that people use to make soap.
3 A kind of tree that is useful for people.
4 A kind of insect that eats everything.

(2) ①②③④

英検３級でよく出る熟語
動詞の熟語

月　日
点

★音声を聞き、声に出して読みながらなぞりましょう。（20点）

♪47

電気をつけてくれる？
Can you turn on the light?

彼は上着を着て、出かけました。
He put on a jacket and went out.

そのネコは私を見て、にげました。
The cat looked at me and ran away.

ボブは私の仕事を手伝ってくれました。
Bob helped me with my work.

あなたに会えるのを楽しみにしています。
I look forward to seeing you.

私に手を貸してください。
Please give me a hand.

お父さんが車でむかえに来てくれました。
My father picked me up.

1 次の(1)と(2)の（　　）に入れるのに最も適切なものを1、2、3、4の中から一つ選び、その番号のマーク欄をぬりつぶしましょう。(10点×2)

(1) ***A :*** The soccer game will start soon.
Please (　　　) on the TV, Mike.
B : Sure.

1 hurt　**2** turn
3 enter　**4** meet

(1) ① ② ③ ④

(2) ***A :*** Did you carry the chairs here alone?
B : No. Asuka gave me a (　　　).

1 nose　**2** leg
3 hand　**4** neck

(2) ① ② ③ ④

2 対話と質問を聞き、その答えとして最も適切なものを1、2、3、4の中から一つ選びましょう。(5点×2)

♪ 48

(1)
1 Buy a cap.
2 Plan a trip.
3 Make sandwiches.
4 Go camping.

(1) ① ② ③ ④

(2)
1 The man.
2 The woman.
3 Ken.
4 Her teacher.

(2) ① ② ③ ④

まとめテスト❶

月　日

点

1 次の(1)から(5)までの（　）に入れるのに最も適切なものを1、2、3、4の中から一つ選び、その番号のマーク欄をぬりつぶしなさい。(8点×5)

(1) ***A*:** I think we should practice more.
***B*:** I (　　) with you. The contest will be soon.

1 forget　　2 imagine
3 agree　　4 guess

(1) ① ② ③ ④

(2) ***A*:** Hi, David. This is Lisa. Are you busy?
***B*:** No. I've just (　　) lunch.

1 finish　　2 finished
3 finishing　　4 to finish

(2) ① ② ③ ④

(3) ***A*:** What does your brother do?
***B*:** He works at a company (　　) makes robots.

1 this　　2 that
3 it　　4 what

(3) ① ② ③ ④

(4) When Kate joined the music club, she didn't know (　　) to play the flute. Now, she sometimes teaches other members.

1 what　　2 whose
3 which　　4 how

(4) ① ② ③ ④

(5) ***A*:** Who is the girl (　　) pictures over there?
***B*:** She's Julia. She's in the newspaper club.

1 take　　2 to take
3 taking　　4 taken

(5) ① ② ③ ④

2 次の(1)から(4)の会話について、(　　)に入れるのに最も適切なものを 1、2、3、4 の中から一つ選び、その番号のマーク欄をぬりつぶしなさい。(15点×4)

(1) ***Salesclerk :*** How about this shirt?

Woman : Hmm, (　　　) I think it's a little too small for me.

1 do you have a bigger one?
2 may I try it on?
3 would you like some?
4 have you got it yet?

(1) ① ② ③ ④

(2) ***Girl 1 :*** Why don't we go to the movies this weekend?

Girl 2 : (　　　) Let's check what we can see.

1 Not yet.
2 Good idea.
3 Maybe next time.
4 Well done.

(2) ① ② ③ ④

(3) ***Woman :*** You look busy. (　　　)

Man : That's OK. I'll finish soon.

1 Can you lend me some money?
2 How do you like it?
3 Do you want me to help you?
4 Have you been there?

(3) ① ② ③ ④

(4) ***Woman :*** Excuse me. (　　　) I think it's around here.

Man : It's on the next street.

1 Do you know where the theater is?
2 Is there a big park in your town?
3 When did you arrive here?
4 Could you help me?

(4) ① ② ③ ④

まとめテスト❷

月　日
点

1 次の掲示の内容に関して、(1)と(2)の質問に対する答えとして最も適切なもの、または文を完成させるのに最も適切なものを 1、2、3、4 の中から一つ選び、その番号のマーク欄をぬりつぶしなさい。(25点×2)

Enjoy music!

Swan City Music Festival will be held on October 15. Enjoy various kinds of music around the city. There will also be some special events.

Dance lesson for kids : At Swan High School gym, 10:30 - 12:30
Hip-hop dancers will teach children how to dance. Children from 5 to 12 years of age can join.

Chorus contest : At Lakeside Hall, 14:00 - 16:00
Eight groups will take part in the contest. Enjoy wonderful songs and give a point to your favorite group.

Special concert : At Greenwood Park, 17:30 - 19:30
At the end of the festival, a famous jazz band, Swings, will give their performance. They are from Swan City and happy to play in their home city.

(1) Children can't take the dance lesson if they

1 don't live in Swan City.
2 have no dance experience.
3 don't have a ticket.
4 are 4 years old or younger.

(1) ① ② ③ ④

(2) What will happen at the park in Swan City on October 15?

1 Some groups will sing songs.
2 Kid dancers will perform.
3 There will be a jazz concert.
4 People will choose the best singer.

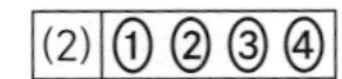

2 次の手紙の内容に関して、(1)と(2)の質問に対する答えとして最も適切なもの、または文を完成させるのに最も適切なものを 1、2、3、4 の中から一つ選び、その番号のマーク欄をぬりつぶしなさい。(25点×2)

June 20

Dear Grandma and Grandpa,

How are you? I had a great time at your house in spring. I really liked Grandpa's apple pie. I also enjoyed picking vegetables with Grandma in the garden. The dishes using fresh vegetables were delicious. And thank you again for the bag you bought me. I use it when I go to piano lessons.

Next month, I'll visit my best friend, Grace. She moved to another city two years ago. I'm excited about meeting her. I'll stay at her house for three days. She lives near a beach, and I'll try surfing with her. Grace has gone surfing a few times, but it'll be my first time. Also, her father is planning to take us to a big amusement park. I'm looking forward to the trip. I'll send you a postcard.

Take care,
Emily

(1) When she visited her grandparents, Emily

1 ate her grandfather's apple pie.
2 bought a bag for her grandmother.
3 played the piano for them.
4 grew vegetables in their garden.

(1) ① ② ③ ④

(2) What is Emily going to do with Grace's father?

1 Write a postcard.
2 Take a surfing lesson.
3 Go to an amusement park.
4 Have a party for Grace.

(2) ① ② ③ ④

まとめテスト③

月　日
点

1 次の英文の内容に関して、(1)と(2)の質問に対する答えとして最も適切なもの、または文を完成させるのに最も適切なものを 1、2、3、4 の中から一つ選び、その番号のマーク欄をぬりつぶしなさい。(25点×2)

Caroline Herschel

Caroline Herschel was born in Germany in 1750. At the age of ten, she became ill, and because of that, she did not grow tall enough. Her parents didn't think that she could find a husband, and her mother believed that she should be a housekeeper* for the family. Herschel couldn't study a lot because she had to work for a long time.

In 1772, Herschel moved to England to live with her brother William. At that time, William was working as a music teacher and an organist* at a church. Herschel did housework to support her brother and also took singing, English, and math lessons from him. She learned how to play the harpsichord,* too. A few years later, she started performing at William's concerts as a singer and became popular.

*housekeeper：家政婦　*organist：オルガン奏者　*harpsichord：ハープシコード（ピアノに似た楽器）

(1) Why couldn't Herschel study a lot when she was young?

1 She worked too long.
2 She often became sick.
3 Her father didn't have enough money.
4 Her parents couldn't find a teacher.

(1) ① ② ③ ④

(2) In England, Herschel

1 taught the harpsichord.
2 became a popular singer.
3 worked as an English teacher.
4 helped people at a church.

(2) ① ② ③ ④

2 次の英文（**1**の続き）の内容に関して、(1)と(2)の質問に対する答えとして最も適切なものを 1、2、3、4 の中から一つ選び、その番号のマーク欄をぬりつぶしなさい。(25点×2)

William was a musician, but he was also very interested in astronomy.* Herschel was trained to be not only a singer but also his assistant in his astronomy work. She helped William to make a telescope* and to observe* stars. In 1781, William discovered Uranus.* It was a big discovery, and he became an astronomer for the king. Herschel stopped her musical career to assist her brother.

Herschell observed stars by herself, too, and made some important discoveries. In 1783, she made her first discovery, a new nebula.* In 1786, she found a comet*. It was the first comet discovered by a woman. Next year, the king decided to pay her 50 pounds a year for her work. Herschel was the first woman who was paid as an astronomer.

*astronomy：天文学　*telescope：望遠鏡　*observe：～を観測する
*Uranus：天王星　*nebula：星雲　*comet：すい星

(1) What happened in 1781?

1 William became successful as a musician.
2 Herschel made her own telescope.
3 William made a big discovery.
4 Herschel received money from the king.

(1) ① ② ③ ④

(2) What is this story about?

1 The king of England in the 18th century.
2 A woman who did great work in astronomy.
3 A special telescope to see comets.
4 How to become a good singer.

(2) ① ② ③ ④

まとめテスト④

月　日

点

1 ライティング（50点）

- あなたは、外国人の友達から以下のQUESTIONをされました。
- QUESTIONについて、あなたの考えとその理由を2つ英文で書きなさい。
- 語数の目安は25語～35語です。
- 解答は、以下の解答欄に書きなさい。
- 解答がQUESTIONに対応していないと判断された場合は、0点と採点されることがあります。QUESTIONをよく読んでから答えてください。

QUESTION

What month of the year do you like the best?

2 ライティング（50点）

- あなたは、外国人の友達から以下のQUESTIONをされました。
- QUESTIONについて、あなたの考えとその理由を2つ英文で書きなさい。
- 語数の目安は25語～35語です。
- 解答は、以下の解答欄に書きなさい。
- 解答がQUESTIONに対応していないと判断された場合は、0点と採点されることがあります。QUESTIONをよく読んでから答えてください。

QUESTION

Which do you like better, playing sports or watching sports?

まとめテスト⑤

月　日

点

1 イラストを参考にしながら対話と応答を聞き、最も適切な応答を 1、2、3 の中から一つ選びなさい。(5点×6)

♪ 49

(1)

(1) ① ② ③

(2)

(2) ① ② ③

(3)

(3) ① ② ③

(4)

(4) ① ② ③

(5)

(5) ① ② ③

(6)

(6) ① ② ③

2 対話と質問を聞き、その答えとして最も適切なものを 1、2、3、4 の中から一つ選びなさい。（10点×4）

♪ 50

(1)
1 To Bob's house.
2 To a shopping mall.
3 To a restaurant.
4 To a flower shop.

(1) ① ② ③ ④

(2)
1 She went to a festival.
2 She did her homework.
3 She enjoyed talking with the boy.
4 She took care of her sister.

(2) ① ② ③ ④

(3)
1 Play the violin.
2 Call her back.
3 Bring her book.
4 Talk to her father.

(3) ① ② ③ ④

(4)
1 The boy won the contest.
2 They met the boy's grandparents.
3 They'll go to the beach.
4 The summer vacation will start soon.

(4) ① ② ③ ④

3 英文と質問を聞き、その答えとして最も適切なものを 1、2、3、4 の中から一つ選びなさい。（15点×2）

♪ 51

(1)
1 A red bag.
2 A yellow bag.
3 A white dress.
4 A blue dress.

(1) ① ② ③ ④

(2)
1 Once a week.
2 Three times a week.
3 Every day.
4 Twice a month.

(2) ① ② ③ ④

答えのページ

まちがえた問題はくりかえし練習しよう！

おさらいテスト ①

1 (1) ③　(2) ②　(3) ①　(4) ②
2 (1) ②　(2) ④　(3) ③
3 (1) ②　(2) ①

1 (1) A：ルーク、どこにいたの？　B：図書室に。宿題をしていたんだ。

解説 was[were] ～ingは「～していた」。

(2) A：新しい自転車がほしいな。　B：見て。私の自転車はあなたのよりも古いよ。
1　古い　2　もっと古い　3　いちばん古い　4　いちばんよい

解説 すぐ後にthan（～より）があるので、「もっと古い」を表す2が適切。

(3) ケンタは、お母さんが病気だったので昨日は早く帰らなければなりませんでした。

解説 had to ～ は「～しなければならなかった」。「～」には過去を表す形ではなく、もとの形の動詞がくる。

(4) A：パーティーでは楽しいときを過ごした？　B：うん。友達と歌って楽しんだよ。

解説 enjoy ～ingは「～することを楽しむ」。enjoyの後にto ～はこない。

2 (1) 息子：おばあちゃんのためにこの絵をかいたよ。　母親：わあ、あなたは絵をかくのが得意だね。とてもすてきに見えるよ。
1　私は彼女に電話しないよ。　3　彼女は手伝いが必要だよ。　4　それはかべにかかっているよ。

解説 look ～は「～に見える」。lookの後には様子を表す言葉を続ける。

(2) 少女1：もうすぐ5時だよ。　少女2：あ、行かなくちゃ。今日はお父さんと夕食を作るの。　1　あなたの時計はいいね。　2　私たちは走っていたよ。　3　あなたはそれをできないよ。

解説 mustは「～しなければならない」という意味。

(3) 女性：今日の午後は何をしたい？　男性：ええと、映画を見るのはどう？　女性：いいね。　1　いくつほしい？　2　どのくらいの長さだった？　4　どうやって来たの？

解説 How about ～ing …?は「～するのはどうですか。」という意味。

リスニング

3 (1) *A:* What do you usually do on weekends?　*B:* I play tennis with my friends.　*A:* What do you do when it rains?　1. I need a new umbrella.　2. I read books at home.　3. It'll be sunny tomorrow.

A：きみは週末、たいてい何をするの？　B：友達とテニスをするよ。　A：雨が降るときは何をするの？　1　私には新しいかさが必要だよ。　2　家で本を読むよ。　3　明日は晴れるよ。

解説 whenは「～するときに」という意味も表す。雨が降るときに何をするかを聞かれているので、応答は2が適切。

(2) *A:* Are you busy tomorrow?　*B:* No, I'm free.　*A:* Can we meet then?　1. Sure, let's have lunch together.　2. Here you are.　3. Well, I don't have time.

A：明日はいそがしい？　B：いいえ、ひまだよ。　A：じゃあ会わない？　1　もちろん、いっしょにランチを食べよう。　2　はい、どうぞ。　3　ええと、時間がないんだ。

おさらいテスト ②

1 (1)② (2)① (3)② (4)③
2 (1)② (2)④
3 (1)② (2)③ (3)④

1 *(1)* A：今日は手伝ってくれてありがとう。　B：どういたしまして。

解説 thank you for ～ingは「～してくれてありがとう」。

(2) リサは駅で古い友人と会ってうれしかった。

解説 be happy to ～は「～してうれしい」。

(3) A：あなたはフランス語が話せるの？　B：うん、少し。子どものときにパリに住んでいたんだ。　1 もし～ならば　2 ～するときに　3 だれ　4 ～だから

(4) A：この美術館には美しい絵がたくさんあるね。　B：うん。私はこれが全部の中でいちばんいいと思う。すごく気に入っているよ。　1 よい　2 もっとよい　3 いちばんよい　4 もっと多い

解説 of allは「全部の中で」。「いちばんよい」を表す3を入れると意味が通る。

2 *(1)* What are you going to do (this weekend?)

解説 Whatの後がare youとなることに注意。

(2) My aunt gave me this watch last (month.)

解説 〈give A B〉で「AにBをあたえる」。

リスニング

3 *(1)* *A:* I have a brother. *B:* Is he older than you? *A:* Yes. He's two years older. *B:* Then he's younger than my sister. Question: Who is two years older than the girl?

A：私には男のきょうだいがいるよ。　B：彼はきみより年上？　A：うん。2さい年上だよ。　B：じゃあ彼はぼくの姉[妹]より年下だね。　質問：だれが少女より2さい年上ですか。　1 少年。　2 少女の兄。　3 少年の姉[妹]。　4 少女の姉。

(2) *A:* Emma, let's go to the shopping mall next Sunday. *B:* Why, Dad? *A:* Your racket is too old. I'll buy you a new one. *B:* Oh, thank you.
Question: Why will they go to the shopping mall next Sunday?

A：エマ、次の日曜日にショッピングモールに行こう。　B：どうして、お父さん？　A：きみのラケットは古すぎるよ。きみに新しいのを買ってあげる。　B：わ、ありがとう。　質問：なぜ彼らは次の日曜日にショッピングモールに行くのですか。　1 映画を見るため。　2 有名なカフェを訪れるため。　3 新しいラケットを買うため。　4 クリスマスのプレゼントを買うため。

解説 まず父親(A)が「ショッピングモールに行こう」と言い、その後に、むすめのラケットが古すぎるから新しいものを買ってあげると言っているので、3が適切。

(3) *A:* Mom, do I need to go to the supermarket? *B:* No, you don't have to. But can you help me in the kitchen? *A:* OK. But can I call Jim first? I'll be quick. *B:* Sure.
Question: What will the boy do next?

A：お母さん、ぼくはスーパーに行く必要がある？　B：いいえ、その必要はないよ。でも台所で私を手伝ってくれる？　A：いいよ。でも先にジムに電話してもいい？　すぐにすませるよ。　B：もちろん。　質問：少年は次に何をしますか。　1 スーパーに行

く。　2　母親を手伝う。　3　昼食を食べる。　4　友達に電話する。

01 何を買えばいいかわからないよ

1 (1)②　(2)③
2 (1)③　(2)④
3 (1)①　(2)③

1 (1) A：放課後、どこに行けばいいか教えてくれる？　B：いいよ。私たちは音楽室に行かなければならないよ。　(2) A：このカメラの使い方を知ってる？　B：うん。あなたに(見せて)教えるよ。　1　何　2　だれ　3　どのように　4　どちら

2 (1) 少年：あれ、きみはグローブを持っているんだね。野球ができるの？　少女：うん。お父さんがプレーのしかたを教えてくれたよ。　1　私は彼にボールを買ったよ。　2　あなたはここでプレーできるよ。　4　私たちの市にある球場は新しいよ。

解説 「野球ができるの？」に対してYes.（うん。）と答えた後に続くので、「父親がプレーのしかたを教えてくれた」と伝えている3が適切。

(2) 男性：どこでチケットを買えばいいか教えていただけますか。　女性：いいですよ。あそこに券売機があります。　1　それは10ドルです。　2　その映画は人気です。　3　次の駅で電車を乗りかえてください。

解説 男性は、where to buy tickets（どこでチケットを買えばよいか）を教えてくれるようにたのんでいるので、券売機の場所を教えている4が適切。

リスニング

3 (1) *A:* Excuse me.　Is that building City Hall?　*B:* No.　It's a museum.　*A:* Oh.　Could you tell me how to get to City Hall?　*B:* Sure.　Just go down this street.　It's next to a post office.　Question: Where does the woman want to go?

A：すみません。あのビルは市役所ですか。　B：いいえ。博物館です。　A：ああ。市役所への行き方を教えていただけますか。　B：いいですよ。この通りを行ってください。郵便局のとなりにあります。　質問：女性はどこに行きたいのですか。　1　市役所。　2　博物館。　3　図書館。　4　郵便局。

(2) *A:* What do we need to buy?　*B:* Wait a minute ....　Oh!　I forgot the shopping list.　*A:* Really?　Then let's call Mom and ask.　*B:* OK.　I'll call her.　Question: What is their problem?

A：私たちは何を買う必要があるの？　B：ちょっと待って…。あ！　買い物リストを忘れた。　A：本当？　じゃあ、お母さんに電話して聞こう。　B：わかった。ぼくが彼女に電話するよ。　質問：彼らの問題は何ですか。
1　彼らは十分なお金を持っていません。
2　彼らは食べ物をたくさん買いすぎました。
3　彼らは何を買えばよいかわかりません。
4　彼らはスーパーを見つけられません。

解説 Bが「買い物リストを忘れた。」と言っているので、それを言いかえた3が適切。

02 カレーを料理するのは簡単だよ

1 (1)③　(2)④
2 ③　3 ②
4 (1)③　(2)④

1 (1) 本を読むことはおもしろいです。
1 これ　2 あれ　3 形式的な主語のit　4 私は　(2) 速く泳ぐことは私にとって難しいです。　1 ～をこえて　2 ～から　3 ～によって　4 ～にとって

2 A：今朝は朝食を食べなかった。　B：えっ、朝食を食べるのは大切だよ。

解説 It's … to ～.で「～することは…です。」を表すので、3が適切。

3 少女：エリック、ちこくだよ。またおそく起きたの？　少年：うん。早く起きるのはぼくには大変なんだよ。　1 昨夜は早くねたんだ。　3 バスが時間通りに来なかったんだ。　4 ぼくはきみが来るすぐ前にここに着いたよ。

解説 おそく起きたのかと聞かれて、少年はYeah.（うん。）と答えているので、早く起きるのは自分には大変だと言っている2が適切。

リスニング

4 (1) *A:* Is that English book yours? *B:* No. It's my sister's. It's hard for me to read English. *A:* Really? But you speak English well. *B:* Oh, thank you.
Question: What is hard for the girl?
A：その英語の本はきみの？　B：ううん。私の姉[妹]の。私には英語を読むことは大変だよ。　A：本当に？　でもきみは英語を上手に話すよ。　B：わ、ありがとう。　質問：少女にとって何が大変ですか。
1 英語を話すことです。　2 物語を書くことです。　3 英語を読むことです。　4 音楽を演奏することです。

(2) *A:* I like soccer. How about you? *B:* Me, too. It's exciting to watch soccer games. *A:* That's right! And the players are really cool. *B:* Yes! My favorite player is Kubota.
Question: Why does the boy like watching soccer?
A：私はサッカーが好き。あなたは？　B：ぼくも。サッカーの試合を見るのはわくわくするよ。　A：その通り！　それに選手たちは本当にかっこいい。　B：うん！　ぼくの大好きな選手はクボタだよ。　質問：なぜ少年はサッカーを見るのが好きなのですか。
1 それはかっこいいです。　2 それは人気があります。　3 それは簡単です。　4 それはわくわくします。

解説 少年は、It's exciting to watch soccer games.（サッカーの試合を見るのはわくわくするよ。）と言っている。

03 重すぎて運べないよ

1	(1) ②	(2) ④
2	(1) ②	(2) ③
3	(1) ②	(2) ③

1 (1) 私はつかれすぎていて走れません。
1 とても　2 ～すぎる　3 ずっと　4 激しく　(2) このお茶は熱すぎて私には飲めません。

2 (1) 少年：きみの弟にこの本はどう？　少女：うーん、何かほかのものを買おうかな。彼は幼すぎてそれを読めないから。　1 それは本当によさそうだね。　3 私はよく彼と図書館に行くよ。　4 わかった、あなたはまた試していいよ。

解説 空所の後のtoo … to ～（…すぎて～できない）を使った文をヒントに考える。

(2) 父親：エマ、これらの野菜を切りに来てくれる？　むすめ：ごめん、いそがしすぎてお父さんを手伝えないよ。　1 私は料

理が得意だよ。　2　私はお店に行けないよ。　4　私はお母さんに電話しなかったよ。

解説 「野菜を切りに来てくれる？」に対してSorry（ごめん）と返答していることから考える。

リスニング

3 (1) I went to the beach with my friends last Sunday. It was too cold to swim in the sea. So we enjoyed playing beach volleyball. Question: What did the boy do when he went to the beach?
ぼくはこの前の日曜日に友達と浜辺に行きました。寒すぎて海では泳げませんでした。それでぼくたちはビーチバレーをして楽しみました。　質問：少年は浜辺に行ったときに何をしましたか。　1　彼はつりを楽しみました。　2　彼はビーチバレーをしました。
3　彼は海で泳ぎました。　4　彼は友達と歩きました。

(2) Yesterday, Jane had math homework, but she was too sleepy to study. So she got up early this morning and did her homework. Question: Why didn't Jane do her homework yesterday?
昨日、ジェーンは数学の宿題がありましたが、ねむすぎて勉強することができませんでした。それで彼女は今朝早く起きて、宿題をしました。　質問：なぜジェーンは昨日、宿題をしなかったのですか。　1　彼女は数学が得意ではありません。　2　彼女の兄［弟］が彼女を手伝いませんでした。
3　彼女はねむすぎました。　4　それはとても難しかったです。

解説 昨日について、she was too sleepy to study（彼女はねむすぎて勉強することができませんでした）と言っている。

04 ギターをひいてほしい

1 (1) ③　(2) ②
2 (1) ③　(2) ①
3 (1) ④　(2) ③

1 (1) 私は彼にルールを説明してくれるようにたのみました。　(2) 私のお母さんは私に部屋をそうじするように言いました。
1　(〜と)言った　2　(人に〜するように)言った　3　しゃべった　4　話した

2 (1) 妹［姉］：公園に行ってサッカーをしようよ。　兄［弟］：ごめん、いそがしいんだ。お父さんがぼくに宿題をするように言ったんだ。　1　うん、そうしよう。
2　ありがとう、ぼくはサッカーが好きだよ。
4　ううん、ぼくたちはする必要はないよ。

解説 空所の後の文をヒントに考える。told me to 〜で「私に〜するように言った」。

(2) 母親：あなたの音楽祭は次の金曜日だね。　息子：うん。おばあちゃんに電話するよ。彼女に来てほしいんだ。　2　ぼくはピアノがひけるよ。　3　彼女はダンスのレッスンがあるよ。　4　彼女は料理が上手だよ。

解説 音楽祭の話が出て、「おばあちゃんに電話する」と言っていることから考える。want her to 〜で「彼女に〜してほしい」。

リスニング

3 (1) *A:* Emily, can you teach me English? I have a test next week. *B:* OK, Makoto. Let's study at the library this weekend. *A:* Thank you.
B: You're welcome. Question: What does Makoto ask Emily to do?
A：エミリー、ぼくに英語を教えてくれる？来週、テストがあるんだ。　B：いいよ、マ

コト。この週末に図書館で勉強しよう。
A：ありがとう。　B：どういたしまして。
質問：マコトはエミリーに何をするようにたのんでいますか。　1　図書館に来る。
2　テストを作る。　3　彼と遊ぶ。
4　彼に英語を教える。

(2) *A:* Hello?　*B:* Hi, Mike. This is Alice. Are you with Mom?　*A:* Yes. We're going to the supermarket.　*B:* Good. Please ask her to get some oranges.
Question: What does Alice want her mother to do?
A：もしもし？　B：もしもし、マイク。アリスだよ。お母さんといっしょにいる？　A：うん。ぼくたち、スーパーマーケットに行くところだよ。　B：よかった。彼女にオレンジをいくつか買うようにたのんで。　質問：アリスはお母さんに何をしてほしいのですか。
1　彼女に電話をかけなおす。　2　彼女のお父さんと話す。　3　オレンジをいくつか買う。　4　マイクをお店に連れていく。
解説　アリスはマイクに、Please ask her to get some oranges.（彼女（=お母さん）にオレンジをいくつか買うようにたのんで。）と言っている。

05 英検3級でよく出る単語①

1 (1) ④　(2) ①
2 (1) ②　(2) ③

1 (1) マサトは4月に高校に行き始めました。彼は音楽が好きなので、学校のバンドに入りました。　1　育てた　2　救った　3　（会などを）開いた　4　参加した
解説　空所の後がthe school band（学校のバンド）なので、4が適切。

(2) A：お母さん、明日アンと買い物に行くよ。　B：わかった、でもお金を使いすぎないようにね。あなたは先週、新しいスカートを買ったばかりでしょ。　1　（お金などを）使う　2　上がる　3　起こる　4　建てる
解説　空所の後がtoo much money（多すぎるお金）なので、1が適切。

リスニング

2 (1) *A:* The next class is science.　*B:* Yeah. Let's go to the science room.　*A:* Oh, I forgot my textbook.　1. It's my favorite subject.　2. Maybe you can borrow Mary's.　3. Ms. Brown will be late.
A：次の授業は理科だよ。　B：うん。理科室に行こう。　A：あ、教科書を忘れた。
1　それは私が大好きな教科だよ。
2　たぶんあなたはメアリーのを借りられるよ。
3　ブラウン先生はおくれるよ。

(2) *A:* You're a member of the basketball team, right?　*B:* Yes. We had a game last week.　*A:* How was it?　1. I'm good at dribbling.　2. It'll start at 4 p.m.　3. It was tough, but we won.
A：あなたはバスケットボール部の部員だよね？　B：うん。先週、試合があったんだ。
A：どうだった？　1　ぼくはドリブルが得意だよ。　2　それは午後4時に始まるよ。　3　大変だったけど、ぼくたちは勝ったよ。
解説　Bが「試合があった」と言ったことに対して、Aが「どうだった？」と聞いているので、試合の感想と結果を伝えている3が適切。wonは「勝った」という意味。

06 500年前に建てられたよ

1 (1)④ (2)③
2 ② 3 ①
4 (1)② (2)③

1 (1) この本は英語で書かれています。
(2) この絵はピカソによってかかれたのですか。

2 A：この歌手は有名ですか。 B：はい。彼は国中で知られています。

解説 有名かと聞かれて、Yes.（はい。）と答えているので、「(国中で)知られている」となるようにする。He's knownで「彼は知られている」。

3 男性：ジュリア、これは日本の料理です。牛どんと呼ばれています。 女性：ああ、私はその名前を知っています。インターネットで見ました。 2 私は彼にも電話しました。 3 私は日本語を話せません。 4 そうですね、私は料理することが好きです。

解説 空所の直前が「それは牛どんと呼ばれています。」で、後が「それをインターネットで見ました。」という流れから、1が適切。

リスニング

4 (1) *A:* Akira, is this museum new? *B:* Well, the guidebook says it was built 15 years ago. *A:* I see. How many pictures can we see here? *B:* About 120. Question: How old is the museum?
A：アキラ、この美術館は新しいの？ B：ええと、ガイドブックには15年前に建てられたとあるよ。 A：なるほど。ここではいくつの絵が見られるの？ B：約120だよ。 質問：美術館はできてからどのくらいですか。
1 できてから5年です。 2 できてから15年です。 3 できてから20年です。
4 できてから120年です。

(2) *A:* You look sad, Lisa. What's wrong? *B:* Someone stole my bike yesterday. *A:* Oh, really? That was a present from your parents. *B:* Yes. I had to take a bus to school today. Question: Why is Lisa sad?
A：悲しそうだね、リサ。どうしたの？ B：昨日、だれかが私の自転車をぬすんだの。 A：え、本当？ あれはご両親からのプレゼントだったよね。 B：そう。今日はバスに乗って学校に来なければならなかったよ。 質問：なぜリサは悲しいのですか。
1 彼女はプレゼントを気に入っていません。
2 彼女はバスに乗れませんでした。
3 彼女の自転車がぬすまれました。
4 彼女の両親が病気です。

解説 リサが言っている、Someone stole my bike（だれかが私の自転車をぬすんだ）を、3ではHer bike was stolen.（彼女の自転車がぬすまれた。）と言いかえている。

07 もう宿題を終えたよ

1 (1)③ (2)②
2 ② 3 ④
4 (1)③ (2)②

1 (1) ケイトはもう家に帰りました。
(2) A：あなたはもうあの映画を見ましたか。
B：いいえ、まだです。

2 A：私たち、夕食後のデザートに果物がいくらか必要だよ。 B：ぼくがもうりんごをいくつか買ったよ。テーブルの上のかごに入っているよ。 1 あとで 2 もう、

すでに　3　まだ　4　上の方へ

解説 Aが「果物が必要」と言ったのに対して、I've ... bought「ぼくが…買った」と答えていることから、2が適切。

3 女性：あなたはもう昼食を食べましたか。　男性：まだです。とてもおなかがすいています。　1　もちろんです。　2　カフェで。　3　ああ、わかりました。

解説 昼食を食べたか聞かれて、空所の後で「おなかがすいている」と言っているので、4が適切。not yetは「まだ(～していない)」。

リスニング

4 *(1)* *A:* Have you visited the new Italian restaurant yet? *B:* No. But my sister went there last night. *A:* What did she say? *B:* She said the pizza was great. Question: Who went to the new restaurant?

A：あなたはもう新しいイタリア料理のレストランをおとずれましたか。　B：いいえ。でも姉[妹]が昨夜、そこへ行きました。　A：彼女は何と言っていましたか。　B：ピザがとてもおいしいと言っていました。　質問：だれが新しいレストランに行きましたか。

1　男性です。　2　女性です。

3　男性の姉[妹]です。　4　女性の姉[妹]です。

(2) *A:* Billy, are you still waiting for the bus? *B:* Yes. It hasn't come yet. *A:* I think it's better to walk to the station. *B:* Maybe you're right.

Question: What is the problem?

A：ビリー、まだバスを待っているの？　B：うん。まだ来ないんだ。　A：駅まで歩くほうがいいと思う。　B：たぶんその通りだね。

質問：何が問題ですか。　1　駅が混んでいます。　2　バスがおくれています。

3　ビリーの友達が来ませんでした。

4　ビリーは一生けんめい働かなければなりません。

解説 ビリーがIt hasn't come yet.（それ(＝バス)がまだ来ないんだ。）と言っている。

08 行ったことがあるよ

1 *(1)*④	*(2)*①
2 ③	3 ②
4 *(1)*①	*(2)*②

1 *(1)* 私はイルカを見たことが一度もありません。　*(2)* あなたはこれまでにカナダに行ったことがありますか。

2 A：あなたはこれまでに韓国料理を食べてみたことがありますか。　B：はい！　何度も食べたことがあります。

解説 空所の前がI'veなので、3が適切。

3 少年1：ぼくのおじさんはオーストラリアに住んでいるよ。　少年2：あ、ぼくはそこに一度行ったことがあるよ。動物園でコアラをだいたよ。　1　いつかそこをおとずれたいな。　3　ぼくにもおじさんがいるよ。

4　ぼくはパスポートが必要だ。

解説「オーストラリア」と聞いて、空所の後で「コアラをだいた」と言っていることから、2が適切。

リスニング

4 *(1)* *A:* Where are you going, Tracy? *B:* To the library to study. *A:* I see. Don't be late for dinner. 1. I'll be back by six. 2. I've been there before. 3. I need some books.

A：どこに行くの、トレイシー？　B：勉強をしに図書館へ。　A：わかった。夕食におくれないでね。　1　6時までにもどるよ。

2 前にそこへ行ったことがあるよ。
3 本が何冊か必要なの。

(2) A: What will you do this weekend? B: I'll go to the beach with my family. A: Have you ever swum in the sea? 1. Yes, you can. 2. Yes, three times. 3. Yes, on the boat.

A：この週末は何をするの？ B：家族と浜辺に行くよ。 A：これまでに海で泳いだことはある？ 1 うん、あなたはできるよ。 2 うん、3回。 3 うん、ボートの上で。

解説 Have you ever ～?（あなたはこれまでに～したことがありますか。）と聞かれているので、Yes（はい）と答えた後に、経験した回数を言っている2が適切。

09 ずっと寒いね

1	(1) ①	(2) ③
2	②	
3	③	
4	(1) ④	(2) ②

1 (1) 私はこの町に3年間住んでいます。
(2) ケンは今朝からずっと自分の部屋にいます。

2 A：アリスはあなたの友達ですか。 B：はい。私は彼女を10年以上知っています（=彼女と10年以上前から知り合いです）。

解説 空所の前がI'veなので、2が適切。

3 男性：トニーはとてもつかれているように見えます。 女性：ええ。彼は今週ずっといそがしくしています。休みの前に仕事を終わらせなければならないのです。 1 彼は早くねました。 2 彼は自分の車のかぎを探しています。 4 彼は自転車で仕事に来ます。

解説 空所の前後の「トニーはとてもつかれているように見える」と「彼は仕事を終わらせなければならない」から、3が適切。

リスニング

4 (1) Today, Sam didn't go to school. He got sick yesterday, and he's still in bed. His mother will take him to the doctor tomorrow. Question: Why didn't Sam go to school today?

今日、サムは学校に行きませんでした。彼は昨日、具合が悪くなり、今もねています。彼のお母さんは明日、彼を医者に連れていきます。 質問：なぜサムは今日、学校に行かなかったのですか。 1 彼は病院に行かなければなりませんでした。 2 彼はつかれすぎていました。 3 彼はお母さんと働きました。 4 彼は昨日からずっと具合が悪いです。

解説 He got sick yesterday, and he's still in bed.（彼（=サム）は昨日、具合が悪くなり、今もねています。）と言っているので、4が適切。

(2) Judy and I have been good friends since we were children. She is a P.E. teacher, and she often plays sports with her students. We sometimes talk on the phone. Question: Who is the woman talking about?

ジュディーと私は私たちが子どものころからよい友達です。彼女は体育の教師で、よく生徒とスポーツをします。私たちはときどき電話で話します。 質問：女性はだれについて話していますか。 1 彼女の子どもです。 2 彼女の友達です。 3 彼女の生徒です。 4 彼女のおばさんです。

10 英検3級でよく出る単語②

1 (1) ③　(2) ②
2 (1) ④　(2) ②

1 (1) A：この前の週末は何をしたの？ B：お父さんと山に登ったんだ。頂上からの景色がすばらしかったよ。 1 わたした 2 笑った 3 登った 4 分けた

解説 空所の後がa mountain（山）なので、3が適切。

(2) A：ドアのところにいる女の人はだれ？ B：ええと、ぼくはどこかで彼女に会ったことがあると思うけど、彼女の名前を思い出せない。 1 従う 2 思い出す 3 信じる 4 上げる

解説 「会ったことがあると思うけど、彼女の名前を～」という流れから、2が適切。

リスニング

2 (1) *A:* How many people will come to your party? *B:* Eight. I invited ten friends, but two of them are busy. *A:* I see. It'll start at six, right? *B:* That's right. Question: How many people did the woman invite?
A：きみのパーティーには何人が来るの？ B：8人。10人の友達を招待したけれど、彼らのうち2人はいそがしくて。 A：そうか。6時に始まるんだよね。 B：そうだよ。 質問：女性は何人を招待しましたか。
1 2人です。 2 6人です。 3 8人です。 4 10人です。

(2) *A:* Were you talking with Bob on the phone? *B:* Yes. We've decided to go fishing next Sunday. *A:* Sounds nice. I'll visit Aunt Mary that day. *B:* Say hello to her, then. Question: What will the boy do next Sunday?
A：ボブと電話で話していたの？ B：うん。ぼくたち、次の日曜日につりに行くことに決めたんだ。 A：いいね。私はその日、メアリーおばさんを訪ねるよ。 B：じゃあ彼女によろしく言って。 質問：少年は次の日曜日に何をしますか。 1 友達に電話する。 2 つりに行く。 3 おばさんを訪ねる。 4 新しい電話を買う。

解説 BはWe've decided to go fishing next Sunday.（ぼくたち、次の日曜日につりに行くことに決めたんだ。）と言っているので、2が適切。decide to ～は「～することに決める」。

11 ポールと話している子

1 (1) ③　(2) ④
2 ④　3 ②
4 (1) ①　(2) ③

1 (1) ピアノをひいている少女はカナです。
(2) これはロンドンでとられた写真です。

2 A：昨日の夜は何をしたの？ B：ぼくの大好きな歌手に書かれた本を読んだよ。

解説 前のbook（本）を説明する語が入るので、「書かれた」という意味を表す4が適切。

3 少女：あの女の人を見て。 少年：どの女の人？ 少女：青いドレスを着ている人。彼女にすごく似合っているの。
1 彼女は私の歴史の先生だよ。
3 いちばん背が高い人。 4 これは彼女の誕生日パーティーだよ。

解説 空所の後で「彼女にすごく似合っているの。」と言っていることから、2が適切。Itは「青いドレス」のこと。

リスニング

4 (1) *A:* Do you know the man standing

by the door? *B:* Yes. He's Mr. Smith, a new science teacher. *A:* I saw him at the supermarket yesterday. *B:* Maybe he lives near your house. Question: Where is Mr. Smith?
A：ドアのそばに立っている男性を知ってる？ B：うん。彼はスミス先生、新しい理科の先生だよ。 A：昨日、彼をスーパーで見かけたよ。 B：たぶん彼はあなたの家の近くに住んでいるんだね。 質問：スミス先生はどこにいますか。 1 ドアのそばです。 2 理科室です。 3 門のところです。 4 スーパーです。
(2) *A:* My father bought a car made in Japan last weekend. *B:* Oh, cool. Does he often drive? *A:* Yes. He goes to work by car. *B:* I see. Question: What did the girl's father do last weekend?
A：先週末、お父さんが日本製の車を買ったの。 B：わ、いいね。きみのお父さんはよく運転するの？ A：うん。彼は車で仕事に行くよ。 B：そうか。 質問：少女のお父さんは先週末、何をしましたか。
1 彼は日本に行きました。 2 彼は一生けんめい働きました。 3 彼は車を買いました。 4 彼は昼食を作りました。
解説 最初に少女(A)がMy father bought a car made in Japan last weekend.（先週末、お父さんが日本製の車を買ったの。）と言っているので、3が適切。a car made in Japanは「日本で作られた車 → 日本製の車」。

12 パリに住むおば

1 (1) ④ (2) ①
2 ② 3 ③
4 (1) ④ (2) ③

1 (1) 私は中国語を話す少年を知っています。 1 どれ 2 いつ 3 どこ 4 前の「人」を説明するときのwho
(2) これは若い少女たちの間で人気のカフェです。 1 前の「もの」を説明するときのwhich 2 いつ 3 どこ 4 だれ
2 A：きみが沖縄でとった写真を見たいな。 B：わかった。明日持ってくるよ。 1 これ 2 前の「もの・人」を説明するときのthat 3 それ 4 これら
解説 前のpictures（写真）を、thatで始まるまとまりが後ろから説明する形にする。このとき、thatに「あれ」という意味はない。
3 少年：グリーン先生が彼女の授業で歌ったって聞いたよ。 少女：うん。彼女は私がとても好きな歌を歌ったから、私はうれしかった。 1 彼女は英語の先生だ、 2 彼女は音楽室にいた、 4 彼女は上手に泳ぐことができる犬を飼っている、
解説 空所の後が「だから私はうれしかった」なので、うれしかった理由に合う3が適切。
リスニング
4 (1) *A:* Excuse me. Is this the train that goes to the airport? *B:* No. Go to Platform Three. *A:* What time is the next train? *B:* It'll leave at two thirty. Question: Where are they talking?
A：すみません、これは空港に行く電車ですか。 B：いいえ。3番ホームに行ってくださ

い。　A：次の電車は何時ですか。　B：2時30分に出ます。　質問：彼らはどこで話していますか。　1　空港です。　2　レストランです。　3　書店です。　4　駅です。

(2) *A:* What are you reading, Lisa?　*B:* A book I borrowed from the library. It's about Egypt.　*A:* Is it your homework?　*B:* No. I'm interested in the country.　Question: Why is Lisa reading the book?

A：何を読んでいるの、リサ？　B：図書館から借りた本。エジプトについてのものだよ。　A：宿題なの？　B：ううん。この国に興味があるの。　質問：リサはなぜその本を読んでいるのですか。　1　彼女はそれを明日返さなければなりません。　2　それは彼女の宿題です。　3　彼女はエジプトに興味があります。　4　彼女の友達が彼女にそれを貸しました。

解説 リサは、読んでいる本について「エジプトについてのものだよ。」と言い、最後にI'm interested in the country.（この国に興味があるの。）と言っているので、3が適切。

13 ニックネームを教えて

1 (1) ③	(2) ①
2 ②	3 ③
4 (1) ②	(2) ①

1 (1) 私にあなたのノートを見せてくれますか。　1　見える　2　目を向ける　3　見せる　4　（動く物を）じっと見る

(2) その知らせは私を悲しくさせました。　1　（〜を…に）した　2　呼んだ　3　あたえた　4　取った

2 A：私にあなたの赤ペンを貸してくれる？　自分のを忘れたの。　B：いいよ。はい、どうぞ。　1　借りる　2　貸す　3　置く　4　伝える

解説 すぐ後の文で「自分のを忘れたの。」と言っていることから、2が適切。

3 少年：見て。いい写真をとったんだ。リサにEメールで送るよ。　少女：わ、きれいだね！　それは彼女をうれしくさせるよ。　1　ぼくは新しいカメラがほしい。　2　ぼくの姉[妹]はよく美術館に行くよ。　4　ブラウンさんがぼくにそのニュースを教えてくれたよ。

解説 前後の「いい写真をとった」「彼女をうれしくさせる」から、3が適切。send A B（AにBを送る）は、send B to Aと表すことができる。Bがitのときは、いつもこの形。show、give、tell、lendなども同じ。

リスニング

4 (1) *A:* How was Emma's birthday party?　*B:* It was a lot of fun.　*A:* Did you give her your painting?

1. Yes, she's fourteen.　2. Yes, she liked it very much.　3. Yes, I'll buy a present.

A：エマの誕生日パーティーはどうだった？　B：すごく楽しかったよ。　A：彼女にあなたの絵をあげたの？　1　うん、彼女は14さいだよ。　2　うん、彼女はとても気に入っていたよ。　3　うん、ぼくはプレゼントを買うつもりだよ。

(2) *A:* Is that your book?　*B:* Yes. It's a book about animals.　*A:* Oh, I like animals, too.　1. I'll lend it to you, then.　2. Let's meet at the library.　3. It was 10 dollars.

A：それはあなたの本？　B：うん。動物に

ついての本だよ。　A：へえ、私も動物が好きだよ。　1　じゃあ、きみに貸すよ。　2　図書館で会おう。　3　10ドルだったよ。

解説 少年の本が動物についての本だと聞いて、少女が「私も動物が好きだよ。」と言っているので、1が適切。

14 何なのか知ってる？

1	(1) ②		(2) ②
2	①	3	③
4	(1) ④		(2) ②

1 (1) 私はエマがどこに住んでいるか知りません。　1　何　2　どこ　3　いつ　4　だれ　(2) あなたはイヌを飼っていますよね。

2 A：ピーターがいつ大阪に来るか私に教えてください。　B：彼は7月7日に来ます。私は空港で彼をむかえるつもりです。
1　いつ　2　どこ　3　なぜ　4　どう

解説 Bが日にちを答えていることから、1が適切。

3 弟［兄］：おじいちゃんの誕生日はもうすぐだよね？　姉［妹］：うん、来週だよ。彼にプレゼントを買おう。私は彼が何をほしいか知っているよ。　1　私はそれがいつか知らない。　2　彼はパーティーを開いたよ。　4　彼は買い物が好きだよ。

解説 直前で「彼にプレゼントを買おう。」と言っていることから、3が適切。

リスニング

4 (1) *A:* Do you know where Kevin is? *B:* I think he's in the gym.　He has basketball practice. *A:* He wasn't there. *B:* Oh, look.　He's running outside.　Question: Where is Kevin?
A：ケビンがどこにいるか知ってる？　B：彼は体育館にいると思う。彼はバスケットボールの練習があるよ。　A：そこにはいなかったんだ。　B：あ、見て。彼は外を走っているよ。　質問：ケビンはどこにいますか。
1　体育館です。　2　入り口のそばです。　3　スポーツ店です。　4　外です。

(2) *A:* You watched a baseball game in New York, didn't you? *B:* No.　I couldn't get a ticket. *A:* That's too bad. *B:* But I enjoyed a musical.　It was fantastic.　Question: What did the woman do in New York?
A：あなたはニューヨークで野球の試合を見たんですよね？　B：いいえ。チケットが取れなかったんです。　A：それは残念。　B：でも私はミュージカルを楽しみました。すばらしかったです。　質問：女性はニューヨークで何をしましたか。　1　彼女は電車のきっぷを買いました。　2　彼女はミュージカルを見ました。　3　彼女は買い物を楽しみました。　4　彼女は野球の試合を見ました。

解説 女性は最後にI enjoyed a musical「私はミュージカルを楽しみました」と言っているので、2が適切。

15 英検3級でよく出る単語③

1	(1) ④	(2) ③
2	(1) ②	(2) ①

1 (1) A：ぼくは本が好きなんだ。将来、子どものためのお話を書きたい。　B：じゃあ作家になりたいんだね。いい夢だね！
1　料理人　2　技術者　3　デザイ

ナー　4　作家

解説 Aは「将来、お話を書きたい」と言っているので、4が適切。

(2) A：マリア、顔に何かついているよ。鏡を見て。　B：あ、うちの犬の毛だ。ありがとう。　1　毛布　2　さいふ　3　鏡　4　はさみ

解説 直前の「顔に何かついている」から、3が適切。

リスニング

2 (1) Today, I went to the post office and sent two packages. Also, my mom needed 10-cent stamps, so I bought three for her. Question: How many stamps did the girl buy?

今日、私は郵便局に行って、小包を2つ送りました。また、お母さんが10セントの切手が必要だったので、彼女のために3枚買いました。　質問：少女は何枚の切手を買いましたか。　1　2枚です。　2　3枚です。　3　7枚です。　4　10枚です。

(2) My wife and I had a party last Saturday. After breakfast, I started cooking for it, and my wife cleaned the house. My brother came early and set the table. Question: Who cooked for the party?

妻と私はこの前の土曜日にパーティーを開きました。朝食の後、私はそれのために料理をし始めて、妻は家をそうじしました。私の兄[弟]が早く来て、テーブルをセットしてくれました。　質問：だれがパーティーのために料理をしましたか。　1　男性です。　2　男性の妻です。　3　男性の友達です。　4　男性の兄[弟]です。

解説 男性が I started cooking for it（私はそれ(＝パーティー)のために料理をし始めた）と言っているので、1が適切。

16 400メートル泳げたよ

1	(1) ②		(2) ④
2	①	3	②
4	(1) ①		(2) ③

1 (1) 学校におくれてはいけません。
1　(速度が)おそい　2　おくれた　3　金持ちの　4　同じ

(2) 音楽室は生徒でいっぱいでした。
1　(音が)大きい　2　まちがった　3　野生の　4　いっぱいの

2 A：外は暗いよ。　B：うん。空が雲におおわれているね。　1　おおわれて　2　明るい　3　役に立つ　4　かしこい

解説 be covered with ～は「～におおわれている」という意味。

3 女性：会議の準備はできていますか、テッド？　男性：もちろんです。もう売上報告書は書き終えました。　1　あなたは何年もここで働いていますか、　3　あなたは自転車で仕事に行きますか、　4　あなたは出張にあきていましたか、

解説 be ready for ～で「～の準備ができている」という意味。2はたずねる文なのでAreで始まっている。

リスニング

4 (1) *A:* Look. This bread is made from rice. *B:* Oh, your husband can eat it then. *A:* Yes. I'll get some for him. *B:* I'll buy sandwiches for lunch.
Question: What will the woman buy?

A：見て。このパンはお米からできているよ。
B：へえ、じゃあきみのだんなさんはそれを

食べられるね。　A：ええ。彼のためにいくらか買うわ。　B：ぼくはランチ用にサンドイッチを買うよ。　質問：女性は何を買いますか。　1　パンです。　2　サンドイッチです。　3　カレーライスです。　4　ピザです。

(2) A: How was the concert last night? B: It was great! But I couldn't meet my friend. A: Why? B: The hall was filled with people. Question: What did the boy do last night?

A：昨夜のコンサートはどうだった？　B：すごくよかったよ！　でも友達には会えなかったんだ。　A：どうして？　B：ホールが人でいっぱいだったんだ。　質問：少年は昨夜、何をしましたか。　1　彼は友達と話しました。　2　彼はホールをそうじしました。　3　彼はコンサートに行きました。　4　彼は何人かの人を助けました。

解説　少女(A)に昨夜のコンサートはどうだったか聞かれて、少年(B)は「すごくよかった」と答えているので、3が適切。

17 映画に行かない？

1 (1)③　(2)②
2 (1)④　(2)①
3 (1)②　(2)①

1 (1) A：ジムのためにパーティーを開くのはどう？　B：楽しそうだね。　1　どれ　2　いつ　3　(How aboutで)～はどうですか　4　どこ　(2) A：夕食(を食べ)に私の家へ来ませんか。　B：もちろん。ありがとう。

2 (1) 少年：明日、ぼくとテニスをしない？　少女：ぜひしたい。自分のラケットを持っていくね。　1　いいえ、けっこう。　2　うん、いくらかほしいな。　3　あなたはよくやったよ。　(2) 女性1：今週末、買い物に行こうか？　女性2：ごめんなさい、いそがしいの。また別のときに。　2　コーヒーがほしいな。　3　あなたもね。　4　いい考えだね。

解説　Shall we ～?（私たちは～しましょうか。）とさそわれて、「いそがしい」と答えていることから、1が適切。

リスニング

3 (1) A: I baked cookies. B: They look delicious. A: Would you like some? 1. I'm good at cooking, too. 2. I'll have a few, thanks. 3. You can buy them at the store.

A：クッキーを焼いたよ。　B：とてもおいしそうだ。　A：いくつかいかが？　1　ぼくも料理が得意だよ。　2　2、3枚もらうよ、ありがとう。　3　お店でそれらを買えるよ。

解説　Would you like ～?は「～はどうですか。」と食べ物などをすすめるときに使う。

(2) A: I'm going hiking with Emma on Sunday. B: Sounds nice. A: Do you want to come with us? 1. Sorry, I have plans that day. 2. Yes, it's in the mountains. 3. Sure, you can join our team.

A：日曜日にエマとハイキングに行くんだ。　B：いいね。　A：ぼくたちといっしょに来ない？　1　ごめん、その日は予定があるの。　2　うん、それは山にあるよ。　3　もちろん、あなたは私たちのチームに入れるよ。

18 試着してもいいですか？

1 (1)④　(2)①
2 (1)②　(2)③
3 (1)③　(2)②

1 (1) A：ジュリア・ホワイトによって書かれた新しい本を探しています。　B：すみません、それは売り切れています。　1 作られた　2 書かれた　3 行われた　4 （sold outで）売り切れた　(2) A：ご注文をうかがいましょうか。　B：はい。ステーキをサラダ付きでお願いします。
1 注文　2 ナイフ　3 思い出　4 値段
2 (1) 男性：このジャケットはすてきですね。試着してもいいですか。　店員：かしこまりました。こちらへどうぞ。　1 いくらですか。　3 ジャケットはありますか。　4 あちらはどうですか。　(2) 女性：シーフードスパゲッティをいただけますか。　ウエイター：かしこまりました。ほかに何かありますか。　女性：いいえ、それだけです。　1 どうしてしないのですか。　2 あなたに電話しましょうか。　4 たしかですか。
解説 空所の後で、女性が「いいえ、それだけです。」と答えていることから、3が適切。

リスニング

3 (1) *A:* Excuse me. I'm looking for a cap. *B:* We have some over here. How about this blue one or this black one? *A:* Hmm, I'll take the blue one. *B:* Thank you. Question: What will the boy buy?
A：すみません。ぼうしを探しているのですが。　B：こちらにいくつかございます。この青いものか、この黒いものはいかがですか。　A：うーん、青いのを買います。　B：ありがとうございます。　質問：少年は何を買いますか。　1 黒いぼうしです。　2 黒いシャツです。　3 青いぼうしです。　4 青いシャツです。
解説 少年(A)は、ぼうしを探していると言って、その後で「青いのを買います。」と言っているので、3が適切。blue oneのoneは、ここではcapのこと。
(2) *A:* Are you ready to order? *B:* Yes. I'll have chicken curry and bread. *A:* Would you like something to drink? *B:* I'd like a cup of tea. Question: Where are they talking?
A：ご注文はお決まりですか。　B：はい。チキンカレーとパンをいただきます。　A：飲み物はいかがですか。　B：紅茶を1ぱいください。　質問：彼らはどこで話していますか。　1 美術館です。　2 レストランです。　3 郵便局です。　4 スーパーです。

19 病院はありますか？

1 (1)②　(2)③
2 (1)④　(2)②
3 (1)③　(2)②

1 (1) A：このあたりに郵便局はありますか。　B：はい。まっすぐ行って、2つ目の角を左に曲がってください。　1 大いに　2 まっすぐに　3 とつぜん　4 ほとんど　(2) A：市役所がどこにあるか教えてもらえますか。　B：もちろんです。となりのブロックにあります。　1 何　2 いつ　3 どこ　4 どれ
2 (1) 少女：科学博物館に行きたいの。そ

こへはどうやって行ける？　少年：パーク駅まで電車に乗って。　1　そこでは何が見られる？　2　あなたも来ない？　3　あなたの教科書はどこにあるの？

解説 How can I get (to) ～?は「私はどのようにして～へ行けますか。」という意味。

(2) 男性：すみません。スタジアムへの道を教えていただけますか。　女性：すみませんが、わかりません。このあたりの者ではないんです。　1　私は野球ができません。　3　それは去年建てられました。　4　ご親切にありがとうございます。

リスニング

3 (1) *A:* Excuse me. Could you help me? *B:* Sure. *A:* Where is the museum? 1. For about ten minutes. 2. That sounds great. 3. It's just around the corner.

A：すみません。助けていただけますか。B：もちろんです。　A：博物館はどこにありますか。　1　約10分間です。　2　それはいいですね。　3　角を曲がってすぐのところです。

(2) *A:* Are you OK? What's wrong? *B:* I'm looking for the city library. *A:* Go down this street. 1. I have some homework. 2. Thank you for your help. 3. Maybe next time.

A：だいじょうぶですか。どうしましたか。B：市立図書館を探しているんです。　A：この道を行ってください。　1　宿題があるんです。　2　助けてくれてありがとうございます。　3　また次のときに。

解説 行き方を教えてもらったので、お礼を言うのが適切。

20 英検3級でよく出る単語④

1 (1)③　(2)①
2 (1)④　(2)③

1 (1) A：6時までに帰って、夕食後に宿題をするよ。　B：わかった。約束を破ったらだめだよ。　1　意見　2　秘密　3　約束　4　理由

解説 break your promiseは「あなたの約束を破る」という意味。

(2) A：劇場への行き方を教えてもらえますか。　B：もちろんです。この道を2ブロック行ってください。左側にあります。　1　劇場　2　事故　3　予定　4　言語

リスニング

2 (1) *A:* What did you do during the vacation? *B:* I went to Italy. My brother studies art at a college there. *A:* Wow! How was your trip? *B:* Great. I visited a famous church. Question: What did the girl do in Italy?

A：休みの間、何をしたの？　B：イタリアに行ったよ。兄[弟]がそこの大学で美術を勉強しているの。　A：わあ！　旅行はどうだった？　B：すごくよかった。有名な教会を訪れたよ。　質問：少女はイタリアで何をしましたか。　1　彼女は大学に行きました。　2　彼女は美術の授業を受けました。　3　彼女はピザを楽しみました。　4　彼女は教会を訪れました。

(2) *A:* Are you still using the computer? *B:* Yes, I need some information about SDGs. *A:* I read about it in today's newspaper. *B:* Really? I'll check it later. Question: Why is the boy using

the computer?
A：まだコンピューターを使っているの？
B：うん、SDGsについての情報が必要なんだ。　A：今日の新聞でそれについて読んだよ。　B：本当？　あとで見てみるよ。　質問：なぜ少年はコンピューターを使っているのですか。　1　ゲームをするためです。　2　ニュースを読むためです。　3　情報を得るためです。　4　母親を助けるためです。

解説 少年(B)は、I need some information「情報が必要だ」と言っているので、3が適切。

21 ポールをお願いできますか？

1 (1)①　(2)②
2 (1)④　(2)②
3 (1)①　(2)②

1 (1) A：もしもし、ケイトです。ロバートはいますか。　B：やあ、ケイト。少し待ってね。　1　(hold onで)電話を切らずに待つ　2　話す　3　取る　4　急ぐ
(2) A：マナミをお願いできますか。　B：ごめんなさい、彼女は今、外出中です。伝言を残したいですか。　1　機会　2　伝言　3　意味　4　困難

2 (1) 男性：もしもし。ハリスさんをお願いできますか。　女性：かしこまりました。少々お待ちください。　1　よくできました。　2　よい一日を。　3　私はだいじょうぶです。　(2) 少女：もしもし。マイクはいますか。　男性：ごめんね、彼は図書館に行ったよ。伝言を受けようか？　少女：いいえ、いいです。あとでかけ直します。
1　私は本は好きではありません。　3　ええと。　4　それはいいですね。

解説 電話で伝言を受けようかと言われて、「いいえ、いいです。」と答えていることから、2が適切。Can I take a message?（伝言を受けましょうか。）も、I'll call back later.（あとでかけ直します。）もよく使われる表現。

リスニング

3 (1) *A:* Hello?　*B:* Hello, this is Ann. Is Brian home?　*A:* Sorry, he's out right now. He's playing soccer in the park.　*B:* Could you tell him I'll meet him at the station tomorrow?　*A:* Sure.　Question: What will Ann and Brian do tomorrow?
A：もしもし？　B：もしもし、アンです。ブライアンはいますか。　A：ごめんね、彼は今外出中だよ。公園でサッカーをしているんだ。　B：彼に、明日駅で待ち合わせると伝えていただけますか。　A：もちろん。
質問：アンとブライアンは明日、何をしますか。　1　駅で待ち合わせる。　2　彼らのコーチを訪ねる。　3　サッカーをする。　4　公園を走る。
(2) *A:* Hello?　*B:* Hello, this is Tomoya. May I speak to Emily?　*A:* Sorry, she went out for lunch.　Can I take a message?　*B:* Could you tell her to call me back?　*A:* OK.　Question: What does Tomoya want Emily to do?
A：もしもし？　B：もしもし、トモヤです。エミリーをお願いできますか。　A：ごめんね、彼女はランチに出かけたの。伝言を受けましょうか？　B：ぼくに折り返し電話をくれるよう伝えてもらえますか。　A：わかりました。　質問：トモヤはエミリーに何をしてもらいたいのですか。　1　彼といっしょに昼食を食べる。　2　彼に折り返し電話

する。　3　彼にメッセージをくれる。
4　日本語で話す。

解説 トモヤ(B)は、折り返し電話をくれるようにエミリーに伝えることをたのんでいるので、2が適切。call ～ backは「～に折り返し電話する」。

22 意見を書く

1 (例) I like to play tennis in my free time. This is because playing tennis is exciting for me. Also, I want to practice a lot to be a better player. (私は自由な時間にテニスをするのが好きです。これは、テニスをすることは私にとってわくわくするからです。また、私はもっと上手な選手になるためにたくさん練習したいです。) (30語)

2 (例) I like going to the mountains better. This is because I can see beautiful flowers and trees in the mountains. Also, I can enjoy the nice views from the top. (私は山に行くほうが好きです。これは、山ではきれいな花や木を見ることができるからです。また、頂上からのすてきな景色を楽しむこともできます。) (30語)

1

英文の意味

あなたは自由な時間に何をするのが好きですか。

解説 別解例：I like to watch videos on the Internet in my free time. This is because watching videos is a lot of fun. Also, I can learn many things from videos. (私は自由な時間にインターネットで動画を見るのが好きです。これは、動画を見ることはとても楽しいからです。また、動画からたくさんのことを学ぶことができます。) (30語)

2

英文の意味

あなたは山に行くのと浜辺に行くのとでは、どちらのほうが好きですか。

解説 まず、質問への答えを書く。質問の文にあるlike ～ betterを使って答える。その後、This is because ～. (これは～だからです。) やAlso, ～. (また、～。) などを使って、理由を2つ述べる。別解例：I like going to the beach better. This is because I like to swim in the sea very much. Also, I can see a beautiful sunset on the beach. (私は浜辺に行くほうが好きです。これは、私は海で泳ぐことが大好きだからです。また、浜辺では美しい夕焼けを見ることができます。) (29語)

23 Eメールへの返信を書く①

(例) The camping was a lot of fun. It was sunny and warm. I enjoyed fishing in the river the most. (キャンプはとても楽しかったです。晴れて暖かかったです。私は川でのつりを最も楽しみました。) (20語)

英文の意味

こんにちは、
メールをありがとう。あなたが家族とキャンプに行ったと聞きました。それについてもっと知りたいです。天気はどうでしたか。また、あなたは何を最も楽しみましたか。
あなたの友達、
リサ

解説 まず、キャンプについて感想や簡単な説明などを伝えるとよい。その後、2つの質問に答える。語数によっては説明を加えてもよい。別解例：I went to a lake with my family. The weather was nice. I enjoyed seeing a lot of stars at night. They were beautiful.（私は家族と湖に行きました。天気はよかったです。夜にたくさんの星を見ることを楽しみました。きれいでした。）（24語）

24 Eメールへの返信を書く②

（例）Yes, I visited my grandparents in Shizuoka. I stayed at their house for five days. I went to a sushi restaurant with them.（はい、私は静岡にいる祖父母を訪ねました。彼らの家に5日間とまりました。彼らとおすし屋さんに行きました。）（23語）

英文の意味

こんにちは、
メールをありがとう。あなたは休みにあなたのおじいさんとおばあさんを訪ねたのですよね。それについてもっと知りたいです。どれくらい彼らの家にとまりましたか。また、彼らと何をしましたか。
あなたの友達、
グレッグ

解説 まず、祖父母を訪ねたことについて、具体的な場所や感想などを伝えるとよい。その後、2つの質問に答える。語数によっては補足説明をつけてもよい。別解例：I was happy to see my grandparents. I stayed with them for a week. I went shopping with them. They bought me a bag.（私は祖父母に会えてうれしかったです。彼らのところに1週間とまりました。彼らと買い物に行きました。彼らが私にかばんを買ってくれました。）（24語）

25 英検3級でよく出る単語⑤

1 (1)② (2)④
2 (1)② (2)③

1 (1) A：私の授業では英語をたくさん話すようにしてください。まちがえることをこわがらないでください。 B：わかりました、ミラー先生。努力します。 1 おどろいて 2 こわがって 3 わくわくして 4 くつろいだ

解説 be afraid of ～は「～をこわがる」という意味。make a mistakeは「まちがえる、ミスをする」という意味。

(2) A：将来、何をしたい？ B：留学したいな。ほかの文化に興味があるから。
1 最近 2 はっきりと 3 ほとんど 4 外国で

リスニング

2 (1) A: You don't look very happy.
B: I'm nervous about today's English

class. *A:* Why? 1. Ms. Smith is from Canada. 2. I have to make a speech. 3. We'll have a history test.
A：うかない顔をしているね。 B：今日の英語の授業にきんちょうしているんだ。 A：どうして？ 1 スミス先生はカナダ出身だよ。 2 スピーチをしなくちゃいけないんだ。 3 歴史のテストがあるんだ。

(2) *A:* What do you want for dinner? *B:* I want to eat beef stew. *A:* OK, but there isn't enough meat. 1. I like Chinese food better. 2. I've already had dinner. 3. I'll go to the supermarket.
A：夕食は何がいい？ B：ビーフシチューが食べたいな。 A：わかった、でも十分な肉がないな。 1 私は中国料理のほうが好きだよ。 2 もう夕食は食べたよ。 3 私、スーパーに行くよ。

解説 父親(A)が「十分な肉がない」と言っているので、買ってくるという意味の申し出をしている3が適切。

26 掲示・案内

1	(1)③	(2)③
2	(1)④	(2)②

1 (1) 生徒はパーティーで何をすることができますか。 1 ピアノをひく。 2 クリスマスケーキを焼く。 3 軽食を食べる。 4 音楽部に入る。

解説 掲示の3文目に「部員たちはみなさんと楽しい時間を過ごすために、ケーキやクッキー、軽食を作ります。」とある。「楽しい時間を過ごすために」とは、すぐ前の文から、クリスマスパーティーのためにということ。

(2) もし生徒が部員を手伝うことができるなら、彼らは～しなければなりません。 1 グラント先生と歌う。 2 ボランティア団体に入る。 3 ベーカー先生と話す。 4 調理室をそうじする。

英文の意味

パーティーを開きましょう！
クリスマスシーズンがやって来ました。料理部のクリスマスパーティーの時期だということです。部員たちはみなさんと楽しい時間を過ごすために、ケーキやクッキー、軽食を作ります。来ませんか？
時：12月20日 午後3時30分から午後5時30分まで
場所：学校のカフェテリア
パーティーに来たい生徒は、12月17日までに申しこみをするために調理室に来なければなりません。当日、私たちといっしょにテーブルをセットすることができる人が必要です。もしボランティアになれるなら、ベーカー先生と話してください。
パーティーでは音楽のグラント先生がクリスマスの歌を何曲かピアノでひいてくれます。いっしょに歌って楽しみましょう！

2 (1) この掲示は何についてのものですか。 1 7月に展示される特別なカップです。 2 家族の絵のある美術館です。 3 有名な芸術家にあたえられたおくり物です。 4 美術館内にオープンするお店です。

(2) この店で50ドル以上使った人は～を受け取ります。 1 オリジナルのカップ。 2 はがきのセット。 3 10パーセント割引のチケット。 4 無料のTシャツ。

解説 "spend over 50 dollars" を手がかりに英文を読むと、営業時間の表示のすぐ下に同じ表現がある。「50ドル以上使ったら特別なはがきのセットをもらえる」と書いてあるので、2が適切。掲示のgetを、問題ではreceiveと言いかえている。

英文の意味

クレイトン美術館内の新しいお店
7月2日にクレイトン美術館に新しいギフトショップがオープンします。たくさんのオリジナルグッズがあります。ご家族やご友人、みなさん自身のために、Tシャツやカップ、買い物バッグなどのすてきなおくり物を見つけることができます。
営業時間：平日 午前10時から午後7時（月曜日は休業）／週末 午前9時30分から午後7時30分
もし50ドル以上お使いなら、特別なはがきのセットをもらえます。はがきには美術館の美しい絵が印刷されています。
1週間（7月2日から8日）開店セールがあります。すべての品が10パーセント割引で売られます。当館のすばらしい美術作品を楽しむ前や楽しんだ後に、お買い物をお楽しみください。

27 Eメール

1 (1) ②　(2) ④
2 (1) ③　(2) ①

1 (1) ロペス先生はいつ自分の国に帰りますか。　1 5月です。　2 来月です。　3 1週間後です。　4 今日です。
(2) アリソンは何をしたいと思っていますか。
1 デイビッドにロペス先生について伝える。　2 学園祭でおどる。　3 何か特別なものをジョシュにあげる。　4 ロペス先生のためにパーティーを開く。

解説 7・8文目に「彼女（＝ロペス先生）のために何かしたいな。パーティーを開くのはどうかな。」とあるので、4が適切。

英文の意味

送信者：アリソン・プライス
あて先：ジョシュ・モーガン
日付：5月11日
件名：ロペス先生

こんにちは、ジョシュ、
ロペス先生について悲しいニュースを聞いたよ。彼女は来月、自分の国に帰るよ。そのことを知ってた？　デイビッドが今日、私にそのニュースを教えてくれたよ。彼も悲しいって言ってた。彼女のスペイン語の授業はとても楽しいし、私は学園祭で彼女とおどって楽しんだよ。彼女のために何かしたいな。パーティーを開くのはどうかな。準備するのに数週間あるから、何か特別なことができるよ。どう思う？
あなたの友達、
アリソン

2 (1) ジョシュはなぜおどろいているのですか。　1 アリソンが彼にビデオメッセージをくれました。　2 彼は学校でスマートフォンを使えませんでした。　3 彼はニュースを知りませんでした。　4 先生が彼にパーティーについてたずねました。
(2) 明日、ジョシュは～。　1 学校で彼のスマートフォンを使うことについてローガン先生にたずねます。　2 友達とビデオメッセージを作ります。　3 彼の家でのパーティーにデイビッドを招待します。

4　生徒と先生にニュースについてたずねます。

解説 "tomorrow" を手がかりに英文を読むと、本文の最後から3文目に「明日、ローガン先生に聞いてみるよ。」とある。何を聞くかは、すぐ前の文から学校でスマートフォンを使うことについてだとわかる。

英文の意味

送信者：ジョシュ・モーガン
あて先：アリソン・プライス
日付：5月11日
件名：いい考えだね

やあ、アリソン、
ニュースを聞いておどろいているよ。ぼくも彼女の授業が好きだから、彼女がいなくなったらさびしい。パーティーを開くのはいい考えだね！　ぼくたちはビデオメッセージを作ることができると思う。スマートフォンで動画をとるのは簡単だよ。生徒や先生に彼女へメッセージをくれるようにたのもう。でも、学校でぼくのスマートフォンを使っていいかわからない。明日、ローガン先生に聞いてみるよ。もしかしたら、ほかの人にちがう案があるかもしれない。放課後、デイビッドやほかの友達と話そうか？
じゃあまた、
ジョシュ

28 説明文（人物について）

1 (1) ②　　(2) ③
2 (1) ①　　(2) ②

1 (1) アンダーソンはいつカリフォルニアに移りましたか。　1　1866年です。
2　1893年です。　3　1898年です。
4　1902年です。

(2) なぜ路面電車の運転士は外がよく見えなかったのですか。　1　何人かの人が路面電車をきれいにしていました。
2　ニューヨークでは外が暗かったです。
3　前の窓に雪がついていました。
4　彼は目に問題がありました。

解説 第2段落の3文目に「前の窓についている雪のために運転士には外を見るのが大変だったのだ。」とあるので、3が適切。

英文の意味

メアリー・アンダーソン

メアリー・アンダーソンは1866年にアラバマで生まれた。彼女が4さいのときに、父親が亡くなった。アンダーソンと彼女の家族、母親と妹［姉］は父親の土地からお金を得ることができた。1893年に、アンダーソンはカリフォルニアに移って、事業を始めた。彼女は牛のための大きな農場とワインを作るためのぶどう畑を持った。1898年に、アンダーソンは病気のおばを助けるためにアラバマにもどった。

1902年の冬、アンダーソンはニューヨークをおとずれた。そこで路面電車に乗っていたとき、彼女はあることに気づいた。前の窓についている雪のために運転士には外を見るのが大変だったのだ。彼は路面電車を止め、外に出て、手で窓をきれいにしなければならなかった。このことがアンダーソンに運転士の問題を解決するためのアイデアをあたえた。それは窓をきれいにする道具、ワイパーだった。

2 (1) 会社はアンダーソンのワイパーを買いませんでした、なぜなら～からです。
1 車は一般的ではなかった。 2 とても高価だった。 3 運転手用のレバーがついていた。 4 彼らにはもっとよい案があった。

解説 "companies" を手がかりに英文を読むと、第1段落（前からの続きで第3段落）の最後から1・2文目に、アンダーソンの案を買う会社がなく、「たいていの人が車を持っていなかったので」彼らはワイパーをよいものだとは思わなかったと説明されている。車を持つ人があまりいなかったことを、選択肢では「一般的ではなかった」と言いかえている。

(2) 1922年に何がありましたか。 1 アンダーソンが新しいタイプのワイパーを作りました。 2 自動車メーカーがアンダーソンのワイパーを付けた車を作り始めました。 3 アンダーソンが自動車会社で働き始めました。 4 より多くの人が雨の日に運転しませんでした。

英文の意味

アラバマにもどった後、アンダーソンは彼女のワイパーを作り始めた。それにはゴムの付いた棒を動かすためのレバーがあった。運転手は車両の中からレバーを使うことで窓をワイパーできれいにすることができた。アンダーソンは自分の案を売ろうとしたが、それを買う会社はなかった。たいていの人が車を持っていなかったので、彼らはワイパーが自分たちにとってよいものだとは思わなかった。

1922年に、キャデラックという自動車メーカーがアンダーソンのワイパーを彼らの車に付け始めた。そのころは車を運転することがますます一般的になっていたが、人々の車の前の窓をきれいにする方法がなかった。キャデラックはアンダーソンの案を使うのがよいと思った。彼女のワイパーの仕組みは基本的に現在のワイパーと同じである。今日、運転手はアンダーソンのおかげで雨や雪の日に安全に運転することができる。

29 説明文（物事について）

1 (1)④ (2)②
2 (1)② (2)③

1 (1) インドの人々はニームの小枝で何をしますか。 1 彼らは果物を食べます。 2 彼らは庭をきれいに保ちます。 3 彼らは絵をかきます。 4 彼らは歯をきれいにします。

(2) なぜ人々は庭にニームの木を植えるのですか。 1 実がオリーブのような味がします。 2 彼らはその木から薬を作ることができます。 3 彼らはそれをお皿を洗うために使います。 4 その木はとても早く育ちます。

解説 "their yard" を手がかりに英文を読むと、第2段落の3文目に「それでインドでは、人々が庭にこの木を植える。」とある。so（それで、だから）の前が理由になるので、前文を見ると、ニームの木が薬になると説明している。

英文の意味

きせきの木

ニームはインド原産の木だ。早く育ち、約20メートルになる。その花は小さくて白く、実はオリーブに似ている。木のすべての部分が人々の役に立つので、ニームはきせきの木と呼ばれている。インドでは、4500年間ニームの木をさまざまな形で使ってきた。たとえば、ニームの小枝を歯ブラシとして使うことは一般的である。人々はこれらのブラシを使うことで歯を健康的に保つことができる。

インドの人々はニームの木は健康によいと思っている。熱があるときや、病気のときにそれらは薬になることがある。それでインドでは、人々が庭にこの木を植える。その葉やほかの部分はインド料理にも使われる。ニームの葉のお茶もある。それは苦い味がする。

2 (1) 私たちはニームオイルを～ために使うことができます。　1 ガーデニング用の服を作る。　2 こん虫から自分の植物を守る。　3 イナゴの群れをつかまえる。　4 特別なケーキを焼く。

解説 ニームオイルについては第1段落(前からの続きで第3段落)の後半に書かれている。こん虫がきらうニームの葉や小枝を、服などをこん虫から守るために使えると述べた後、「ニームオイルはガーデニングに役立つ。それは植物を守ってくれる。」と説明している。

(2) この話は何についてですか。　1 インドで発熱に使われる薬です。　2 せっけんを作るために人々が使うオイルです。　3 人々の役に立つ木の一種です。　4 すべてのものを食べるこん虫の一種です。

英文の意味

多くの種類のこん虫がニームを好きではない。1959年に、イナゴの大群がスーダンにやって来て、あらゆる植物がそれらに食べられた。しかし、イナゴが去ったあと、野原にはニームの木だけが立っていた。服や食べ物をこん虫から守るためにニームの葉や小枝を使うことができる。また、ニームオイルはガーデニングに役立つ。それは植物を守ってくれる。ニームの実や種からオイルを得ることができる。オイルを取った後の実や種はニームケーキと呼ばれる。ニームケーキを庭の地面に置くのがよい。植物がよく育つ。

ニームせっけんやニームシャンプーなど、ニームを利用するほかの方法もある。ニームにはよい点がたくさんあるので、世界の多くの場所で科学者がそれを研究している。

30 英検3級でよく出る熟語

1 (1) ②　(2) ③

2 (1) ④　(2) ①

1 (1) A：サッカーの試合がもうすぐ始まる。テレビをつけて、マイク。　B：いいよ。　1 傷つける　2 (turn onで)(テレビなどを)つける　3 入る　4 会う

(2) A：ここにあるいすをひとりで運んだの？　B：ううん。アスカが手を貸してくれたよ。　1 鼻　2 あし　3 手　4 首

解説 give ～ a handは「～に手を貸す」。

リスニング

2 (1) *A:* I'm looking forward to the camping trip this weekend. *B:* Me, too. I'll bring my favorite snacks. *A:* I bought a new cap for the trip. *B:* Nice! Question: What will the girl and the boy do this weekend?

A：今週末のキャンプ旅行が楽しみ。　B：ぼくも。ぼくは大好きなおやつを持っていく

よ。　A：私は旅行のために新しいぼうしを買ったよ。　B：いいね！　質問：少女と少年は今週末、何をしますか。　1　ぼうしを買う。　2　旅行を計画する。　3　サンドイッチを作る。　4　キャンプに行く。

(2) *A:* Emma's dance lesson will be over soon. I'll go and pick her up. *B:* I'll go. You look tired. *A:* Oh, thanks. I had a lot of work today because Ken was on vacation. *B:* I see. Question: Who will pick up Emma?

A：エマのダンスのレッスンがもうすぐ終わる。彼女を車でむかえに行ってくる。　B：ぼくが行くよ。きみはつかれているみたいだよ。　A：え、ありがとう。ケンが休暇中だったから今日は仕事がたくさんあったの。B：なるほど。　質問：だれがエマを車でむかえに行きますか。　1　男性です。　2　女性です。　3　ケンです。　4　彼女の先生です。

解説 初めに女性(A)が「彼女を車でむかえに行ってくる。」と言ったが、すぐ後に男性(B)が「ぼくが行くよ。」と申し出て、そうすることになったので、1が適切。

まとめテスト ①

1 (1)③　(2)②　(3)②　(4)④　(5)③
2 (1)①　(2)②　(3)③　(4)①

1 (1) A：私たちはもっと練習するべきだと思う。　B：きみに賛成だよ。コンテストはもうすぐだ。　1　忘れる　2　想像する　3　賛成する　4　推測する

解説 agree with ～は「～に賛成する」。

(2) A：こんにちは、デイビッド。リサだよ。いそがしい？　B：ううん。ちょうど昼ご飯を終えたところだよ。

解説 前にI'veがあるので、2が適切。

(3) A：あなたのお兄さん[弟さん]は何をしているの？　B：彼はロボットを作る会社で働いているよ。　1　これ　2　前の「もの・人」を説明するときのthat　3　それ　4　何

解説 company(会社)をmakes robots (ロボットを作る) が説明する文。ものを説明する場合はwhichまたはthatを使うので、2が適切。人を説明する場合はwhoまたはthatを使う。

(4) ケイトは音楽部に入ったとき、フルートのふき方を知りませんでした。今では、ときどきほかの部員に教えることがあります。
1　何　2　だれの　3　どれ
4　どのように

解説 how to ～は「～のしかた」。what to ～なら「何を～するか」、which to ～なら「どれ[どちら]を～するか」。

(5) A：向こうで写真をとっている少女はだれ？　B：彼女はジュリアだよ。彼女は新聞部に入っているよ。

解説 the girl taking picturesで「写真をとっている少女」。4のtakenはa picture taken in Tokyo (東京でとられた写真) のように使う。

2 (1) 店員：このシャツはいかがですか。女性：うーん、もっと大きいものはありますか。私には少し小さすぎると思います。
2　試着してもいいですか。　3　少しいかがですか。　4　もうそれを手に入れましたか。

解説 すぐ後で「私には少し小さすぎると思う」と言っているので、1が適切。

(2) 少女1：今週末、映画に行かない？

少女2：いい考えだね。何が見られるかチェックしよう。　1　まだだよ。　3　また次のときにね。　4　よくやったよ。

(3) 女性：いそがしそうだね。私に手伝ってほしい？　男性：いいよ。もうすぐ終わるから。　1　お金を貸してくれる？　2　それをどう思う？　4　そこに行ったことはある？

解説 すぐ前の発言から、いそがしそうな人に話しているとわかるので、3が適切。「私が手伝おうか。」と申し出るような意味で言っている。

(4) 女性：すみません。劇場がどこにあるか知っていますか。このあたりにあると思うのですが。　男性：となりの通りにありますよ。
2　あなたの町に大きな公園はありますか。
3　あなたはいつここに着きましたか。
4　助けていただけますか。

解説 男性が場所を答えていることから、1が適切。where ～ is で「どこに～があるか」。

まとめテスト②

1 (1) ④　(2) ③
2 (1) ①　(2) ③

1 (1) もし～なら、子どもたちはダンスレッスンを受けられません。　1　スワン市に住んでいない。　2　ダンスの経験がない。
3　チケットを持っていない。　4　4さいかそれより年下。

(2) 10月15日にスワン市の公園で何が起こりますか。　1　いくつかのグループが歌を歌う。　2　子どものダンサーが公演する。　3　ジャズのコンサートがある。
4　人々がいちばん上手な歌手を選ぶ。

解説 park がキーワード。3つ目に示されているイベントにAt Greenwood Park「グリーンウッド公園にて」とある。イベントはSpecial concertで、jazz bandが公演すると説明されている。

英文の意味

音楽を楽しみましょう！
スワン市音楽祭が10月15日に行われます。市内のあちこちでさまざまな音楽を楽しんでください。いくつかの特別なイベントもあります。
子どものためのダンスレッスン：スワン高校の体育館にて、10:30 - 12:30
ヒップホップダンサーが子どもたちにおどり方を教えます。5さいから12さいまでのお子さんが参加できます。
コーラスコンテスト：レイクサイドホールにて、14:00 - 16:00
8つのグループがコンテストに参加します。すばらしい歌を楽しんで、気に入ったグループに得点を入れてください。
特別なコンサート：グリーンウッド公園にて、17:30 - 19:30
祭りの最後に、有名なジャズバンドのスイングズが公演をします。彼らはスワン市出身で、故郷で演奏することを喜んでいます。

2 (1) 祖父母を訪ねたとき、エミリーは～
1　祖父のアップルパイを食べました。
2　祖母にかばんを買ってあげました。
3　彼らのためにピアノをひきました。
4　彼らの庭で野菜を育てました。

(2) エミリーはグレースの父親と何をする予定ですか。　1　はがきを書きます。
2　サーフィンのレッスンを受けます。
3　遊園地に行きます。　4　グレースのためにパーティーを開きます。

解説 fatherがキーワード。手紙の本文の最後から3文目に「彼女のお父さんが私たちを大きな遊園地に連れていってくれる予定です」とある。

英文の意味

6月20日

親愛なるおばあちゃんとおじいちゃん、

元気ですか。春にはあなたたちの家でとても楽しい時を過ごしました。おじいちゃんのアップルパイを本当に気に入りました。また、庭でおばあちゃんと野菜を採るのを楽しみました。新せんな野菜を使った料理はとてもおいしかったです。それから、私に買ってくれたかばんのこと、改めてありがとう。ピアノのレッスンに行くときに使っています。

来月、私は親友のグレースを訪ねます。彼女は2年前に別の市に引っこしました。彼女に会うことにわくわくしています。彼女の家に3日とまります。彼女はビーチの近くに住んでいて、私は彼女とサーフィンにちょう戦します。グレースは数回サーフィンに行ったことがありますが、私は初めてです。また、彼女のお父さんが私たちを大きな遊園地に連れていってくれる予定です。旅行が楽しみです。はがきを送ります。

体に気をつけて、

エミリー

まとめテスト③

1 (1) ①　(2) ②

2 (1) ③　(2) ②

1 (1) なぜハーシェルは若いときにあまり勉強することができなかったのですか。

1 彼女はあまりに長く働きました。

2 彼女はよく病気になりました。

3 彼女の父親には十分なお金がありませんでした。　4 彼女の両親は先生を見つけられませんでした。

(2) イングランドで、ハーシェルは～

1 ハープシコードを教えました。

2 人気の歌手になりました。　3 英語の教師として働きました。　4 教会で人々を助けました。

解説 第2段落の最後の文に、「彼女は…コンサートに歌手として出演し始め、人気になった」とある。

英文の意味

カロライン・ハーシェル

カロライン・ハーシェルは1750年にドイツで生まれた。10さいのとき、彼女は病気になり、そのために身長が十分にのびなかった。彼女の両親は彼女が夫を見つけられるとは思わず、それで母親は彼女は家族のための家政婦になるべきだと思った。ハーシェルは長い時間働かなければならなかったので、あまり勉強することができなかった。

1772年に、ハーシェルは兄のウィリアムと暮らすためにイングランドに移った。そのころ、ウィリアムは音楽教師と教会のオルガン奏者として働いていた。ハーシェルは兄を支えるために家事をし、また歌と英語と数学のレッスンを彼から受けた。彼女はハープシコードのひき方も学んだ。数年後、彼女はウィリアムのコンサートに歌手として出演し始め、人気になった。

2 (1) 1781年に何がありましたか。
1 ウィリアムが音楽家として成功しました。
2 ハーシェルが自分の望遠鏡を作りました。 3 ウィリアムが大きな発見をしました。 4 ハーシェルが国王からお金を受け取りました。
(2) この話は何についてのものですか。
1 18世紀のイングランドの王です。
2 天文学ですばらしい仕事をした女性です。
3 すい星を見るための特別な望遠鏡です。
4 上手な歌手になる方法です。

解説 この話の話題は、タイトルや最初の文にあるように、カロライン・ハーシェルで、最後の段落では彼女が天文学上のいくつかの重要な発見をしたことが述べられている。

英文の意味

ウィリアムは音楽家だったが、天文学にもとても興味があった。ハーシェルは歌手だけではなく彼の天文学の仕事の助手にもなるために訓練を受けた。彼女はウィリアムが望遠鏡を作ることや星を観測することを手伝った。1781年に、ウィリアムは天王星を発見した。それは大きな発見で、彼は国王のための天文学者になった。ハーシェルは兄を手伝うために音楽の仕事をやめた。

ハーシェルは自分自身でも星を観測し、いくつかの重要な発見をした。1783年に、彼女は最初の発見をし、それは新しい星雲だった。1786年には、彼女はすい星を見つけた。それは女性によって発見された最初のすい星だった。翌年、国王は彼女の仕事に対して年に50ポンドはらうことを決めた。ハーシェルは天文学者として初めて支はらいを受けた女性だった。

まとめテスト④

1 (例) I like October the best. This is because my birthday is in October. Also, the weather is nice and I can enjoy outdoor activities that month.（私は10月がいちばん好きです。これは、私の誕生日が10月にあるからです。また、その月は気候がよく、屋外での活動を楽しめます。）(26語)

2 (例) I like watching sports better. This is because sports games by professional players are really exciting. Also, I'm not good at sports, so playing sports is not fun for me.
（私はスポーツを見るほうが好きです。これは、プロの選手によるスポーツの試合は本当にわくわくするからです。また、私はスポーツが得意ではないので、スポーツをすることは私には楽しくありません。）(30語)

1

英文の意味

あなたは1年の何月がいちばん好きですか。

解説 まず、質問への答えを書く。質問の文にある like ~ the best を使って答える。その後、This is because ~.（これは～だからです。）や Also, ~.（また、～。）などを使って、理由を2つ述べる。別解例：I like August the best. This is because we have a long vacation in August. Also, I can swim in the sea and eat delicious watermelon.（私は8月がいちばん好きです。これは、8月には長い休みがあるからです。また、海で泳いだり、おいしいスイカを食べたりすることができます。）（26語）

2

英文の意味

あなたはスポーツをするのとスポーツを見るのとでは、どちらのほうが好きですか。

解説 別解例：I like playing sports better. This is because playing sports is more exciting for me. Also, I can make good friends if I play with others.（私はスポーツをするほうが好きです。これは、スポーツをすることのほうが私にはわくわくするからです。また、ほかの人とプレーすれば仲のよい友達を作ることができます。）（26語）

まとめテスト⑤

1 (1)② (2)① (3)② (4)①
(5)③ (6)②
2 (1)② (2)④ (3)③ (4)①
3 (1)② (2)①

1 *(1) A:* I visited Spain last month. *B:* Really? I've been there, too. *A:* When did you go? 1. No problem. 2. When I was a student. 3. It was warm.
A：先月、スペインに行ったの。 B：本当？ぼくも行ったことあるよ。 A：いつ行ったの？ 1 問題ないよ。 2 学生のときに。 3 暖かかったよ。

解説「いつ？」とたずねているので、時を答えている2が適切。whenは「いつ」のほか、「～のときに」という意味も表す。

(2) A: Do you have any plans this weekend? *B:* No, nothing special. *A:* Why don't we go hiking? 1. Good idea. 2. Sometimes with friends. 3. Same to you.
A：今週末、何か予定はある？ B：ううん、特に何もないよ。 A：ハイキングに行かない？ 1 いい考えだね。 2 ときどき友達と。 3 きみにも同様に。

解説 提案されているので、賛成を表している1が適切。

(3) A: What's wrong, Kevin? *B:* I don't have a red pen. *A:* You can borrow mine. 1. Sounds like fun. 2. That's nice of you. 3. You'll be OK.
A：どうしたの、ケビン？ B：赤ペンを持っていないんだ。 A：私のを借りていいよ。 1 楽しそうだね。 2 親切にありがとう。 3 きみはだいじょうぶだよ。

解説 That's nice of you.は「親切にありがとう。」という意味。nice の代わりにkindを使うこともある。お礼としてよく言う表現。

(4) A: Are you ready for the trip? *B:* No, not yet. *A:* Where's your passport? 1. I'm not sure. 2. To the airport. 3. It was great.
A：旅行の準備はできている？ B：ううん、まだだよ。 A：パスポートはどこにあるの？ 1 わからない。 2 空港へ。 3 すばらしかったよ。

解説「どこ？」とたずねているが、パスポートがどこにあるかという内容なので、2では対話が成立しない。1の「わからない。」で対話が成立する。

(5) A: May I help you? *B:* Yes. I'm looking for an umbrella. *A:* Sorry, but

we don't sell them. 1. Well, I'll be back. 2. No, it's not mine. 3. OK, thanks anyway.
A：何かお探しですか。 B：はい。かさを探しています。 A：すみません、かさは売っておりません。 1 ええと、もどってきます。 2 いいえ、それは私のものではありません。 3 わかりました、とにかくありがとうございます。
解説 Thanks anyway.（とにかくありがとうございます。）は、求めるものがなかったり、質問の答えを相手が知らなかったりした場合に、それでも自分を手伝ってくれようとしたことに対してお礼を言うときに使う。

(6) *A:* Is that game fun? *B:* Yes. Let's play together. *A:* But I don't know how to play. 1. I want a new one. 2. I'll show you. 3. It wasn't expensive.
A：そのゲームは楽しいの？ B：うん。いっしょにしようよ。 A：でもやり方を知らないよ。 1 新しいのがほしいな。
2 教えてあげる。 3 高くなかったよ。
解説 Aが「やり方を知らない」と言ったことへの応答としては、2が適切。この show は「見せて教える」という意味。

2 *(1)* *A:* I was invited to Bob's birthday party at a restaurant. *B:* Me, too. I don't know what to get for him. *A:* Let's go to the shopping mall together. How about tomorrow? *B:* OK. Question: Where will they go tomorrow?
A：レストランでのボブの誕生日パーティーに招待されたよ。 B：私も。彼に何を買えばいいかわからないな。 A：いっしょにショッピングモールに行こう。明日はどう？ B：いいよ。 質問：彼らは明日、どこに行きますか。 1 ボブの家です。 2 ショッピングモールです。 3 レストランです。
4 生花店です。
解説 少年(A)が「ショッピングモールに行こう」と提案して、少女(B)も同意しているので、2が適切。

(2) *A:* Did you enjoy the festival on the weekend? *B:* Actually, I was too busy to go. *A:* Did you have a lot of homework? *B:* No. I had to take care of my sister. Question: What did the girl do on the weekend?
A：週末、お祭りを楽しんだ？ B：実は、いそがしすぎて行けなかった。 A：宿題がたくさんあったの？ B：ううん。妹［姉］のめんどうを見なければならなかったの。 質問：少女は週末に何をしましたか。
1 彼女はお祭りに行きました。 2 彼女は宿題をしました。 3 彼女は少年と話して楽しみました。 4 彼女は妹［姉］のめんどうを見ました。
解説 少女(B)は最後に「妹［姉］のめんどうを見なければならなかった」と言っている。

(3) *A:* Hello? *B:* Hello, this is Sarah. May I speak to Mark? *A:* Sorry, he went to his violin lesson. May I take a message? *B:* Could you tell him to bring my book tomorrow? *A:* Sure. Question: What does Sarah want Mark to do?
A：もしもし？ B：もしもし、サラです。マークをお願いできますか。 A：ごめんね、彼はバイオリンのレッスンに行ったんだ。伝言を受けようか？ B：明日、私の本を持ってくるように彼に伝えていただけますか。 A：もちろん。 質問：サラはマークに何をして

ほしいのですか。　1　バイオリンをひく。　2　彼女に折り返し電話する。　3　彼女の本を持ってくる。　4　彼女の父親と話す。

解説 サラ(B)は「明日、私の本を持ってくるように彼(=マーク)に伝えていただけますか。」と伝言している。

(4) *A:* Mom, my picture won the contest! *B:* Wow, I'm proud of you! What did you paint? *A:* The beach we visited in summer. *B:* I see. I have to tell your grandpa and grandma.
Question: Why are they happy?

A：お母さん、ぼくの絵がコンテストに勝ったよ!　B：わあ、あなたをほこりに思うよ!　何をかいたの?　A：夏にぼくたちがおとずれた浜辺だよ。　B：なるほど。あなたのおじいちゃんとおばあちゃんにも伝えなくちゃ。
質問：彼らはなぜ喜んでいるのですか。

1　少年がコンテストに勝ちました。
2　彼らは少年の祖父母に会いました。
3　彼らは浜辺に行きます。　4　夏休みがもうすぐ始まります。

解説 少年(A)が最初に「ぼくの絵がコンテストに勝った」と言っている。

3 *(1)* One day, Jane found a nice red bag at a store called Blue Sky. But it was too expensive for her to buy. She also liked a yellow bag and bought that. She thinks it will look nice with her white dress. Question: What did Jane buy?

ある日、ジェーンはブルースカイというお店ですてきな赤いかばんを見つけました。でもそれは高すぎて彼女には買えませんでした。彼女は黄色いかばんも気に入って、それを買いました。彼女は、それは自分の白いドレスに合うだろうと思っています。　質問：ジェーンは何を買いましたか。　1　赤いかばんです。　2　黄色いかばんです。　3　白いドレスです。　4　青いドレスです。

解説 「黄色いかばんも気に入ってそれを買った」と言っているので、2が適切。

(2) I have taken piano lessons for three years. I practice every day and have a lesson every Friday. My piano teacher plays at a restaurant twice a month. Question: How often does the woman take a piano lesson?

私はピアノのレッスンを3年間受けています。毎日練習して、毎週金曜日にレッスンがあります。私のピアノの先生は、月に2回レストランで演奏します。　質問：女性はどれくらいのひん度でピアノのレッスンを受けていますか。　1　週に1回です。　2　週に3回です。　3　毎日です。　4　月に2回です。

解説 「毎週金曜日にレッスンがある」と言っているので、1が適切。